KOKORO
A MEXICAN WOMAN IN JAPAN

By
ARACELI TINAJERO

Title: *Kokoro: A Mexican Woman in Japan*
ISBN-10: 1-940075-47-5
ISBN-13: 978-1-940075-47-1

Design: © Ana Paola González
Cover Design: © Jhon Aguasaco
Cover Image: Yōshū Chikanobu print (1897)
Editor in Chief: Carlos Aguasaco
E-mail: carlos@artepoetica.com / aguasaco@gmail.com
Mail: 38-38 215 Place, Bayside, NY 11361, USA.

Library of Congress Subject Heading:
PQ7081.46.T56 A313 2017
Japan -- Social life and customs -- 21st century.
Japan -- Social life and customs -- 20th century.
Japan -- Description and travel.
Popular culture -- Japan.
Japan -- Social conditions.
Women authors, Latin American -- Japan.
Mexico -- Social life and customs.
Includes photographs.

All photographs are courtesy of the author.

KOKORO
A MEXICAN WOMAN IN JAPAN

BY

ARACELI TINAJERO

TRANSLATED BY

DANIEL SHAPIRO

escribana
books

NEW YORK, 2017

To *Lizeth*

ACKNOWLEDGMENTS

I'd like to thank the people of Japan for their sincere and warm hospitality. I learned so much from the Japanese people that in a thousand years I could never thank them enough for all that they did for me.

I thank my brothers and sisters for their wonderful support. All of them: Ángel, Leticia, Graciela, María Eugenia, Natividad, Elvia, Josefina, Iván, and Lizbeth.

I'm incredibly lucky to have marvelous friends who've always encouraged me to keep writing. Many, many thanks to Ana Botija, Carlos Alberto González Sánchez, Mónica Ricketts, and to Alfonso Quiroz, who unfortunately passed away in 2013 but whose spirit is still with us. I'm also indebted to my dear friend Roberto González Echevarría, who read my work with enthusiasm and suggested the title of this book.

Professor Kato Takahiro, of Nanzan University, read my manuscript with the greatest care, as if under a magnifying glass. Many thanks to him for his time and generosity. I also give thanks to my colleague Kaku Shiyo, who took charge of reviewing all the Japanese words in the book.

I'll always be grateful to Pío E. Serrano, of Editorial Verbum, for his faith in my writing. Thanks to him, the original Spanish-language edition of *Kokoro* was made possible.

I give additional thanks to Esther Allen and Byron Echeverría for their wise advice regarding the publication of this edition.

I'm above all indebted to poet, translator, and essayist Daniel Shapiro for his sensitive translation of this book. During the translation process, we had many unforgettable get-togethers in Manhattan, spending hours discussing Japanese culture. I thank him for his patience throughout.

I'm grateful to Carlos Aguasaco of Artepoética Press for his wisdom, professionalism, and warm reception.

Finally, my deepest gratitude goes to Stephen Pollard. He knows why.

Araceli Tinajero, October 2016

CONTENTS

Kokoro Yasashii
(Tender Heart)

I had to get out of Tokyo. It was only Wednesday, a gentle spring breeze wafted around me, but I was fed up with the city. I'd never seen so many people, even in Mexico City's Pino Suárez station. The rushing to-and-fro in the Tokyo station left me stunned. Women were taking off their high heels and running barefoot so they'd catch their trains. So many uptight-looking faces! I thought of the danger in Mexico City's subway stations but I'd never felt so oppressed. Years before, I'd dreamed about the neighborhood of Roppongi and, just as I'd imagined, its buildings with enormous neon-signs reminded me of what I hadn't yet lived. I always thought that Mexico City was big but Tokyo surprised me not so much by its expanse but by its trains and crowds.

I had a seat by the window. The *Shinkansen* was modern, with velvet-covered seats, a spacious and impeccable train, nothing like the one my father had taken us to Veracruz in. I didn't notice when it began moving but I did begin to feel a lump in my throat. Tokyo had definitely been a mistake. I should have never gone through it. I was desperate to get to Kyoto, that's right, to Kyoto, Kyoto; not Tokyo. I began crying. Suddenly, the typically Japanese houses and rice-fields began appearing. Everything looked crystal-clear and blurry. I'd dreamt of this landscape for so many years but I couldn't stop sobbing. A man in a navy-blue uniform and white gloves entered my car, said something, took off his cap, and bowed. He was the ticket-collector. Even on trains they bow their heads, I thought. We passed through towns and cities and, unbelievably, in the distance, Mount Fuji came into view. I'd always liked seeing the Popo and Ixtla

11

volcanoes at dawn. February was always a dusty, detestable month but the wind made it possible for us to see them more clearly. How lucky to have been born in a valley. When you're born surrounded by mountains, you feel naked if you're not near them. No, photos couldn't capture the beauty of Fuji's perpetual snow. And it looked so close! I should have been happy but my weeping overcame me. I was never one to use handkerchiefs so I wiped off my sadness with my palms.

Vendors were passing by, selling prepared food—snacks, tea, beer, and *sake*. The Japanese language always sounded beautiful to me, even when I didn't understand it. Its tone was always delightful, maybe because it was usually spoken in a soft voice.

"*Ocha wa ikaga desuka?*" I understood what the passenger seated next to me was asking, but how could I answer him without looking him in the eye and how could I tell him no?

"*Do you speak English?*" I felt trapped.

"*Just a little.*"

"*Would you like some tea?*" Looking down, I told him no.

He suddenly took out a beige handkerchief and handed it to me. I accepted it as I became lost once again among the rice-fields. It was true. As much as Tokyo had deceived me, the graciousness of people in the street, in shops, anywhere, also charmed me. From the beginning I felt I-don't-know-what; so much good will almost grieved me. I always felt shy, as if there were some thank-you I'd forgotten to say. I knew about Japanese bowing but it was different experiencing it in the flesh. My mother had brought me up impeccably and had impressed old-fashioned manners on me but from that to Japanese refinement was like the distance from Mexico to China.

The passenger asked me some question. I continued feeling embarrassed and tongue-tied. Surely he'd already studied almost everything about me: my eyes, my nose, my legs. Later I learned that people focused on those features when they weren't sure if I was Japanese or not. On top of that, on a sunny day, it could have occurred only to me to wear moccasins, very short denim shorts, a blue t-shirt that said "Shogun," and a windbreaker; all that to show myself off. He bought *onigiri*, dried squid, peanuts, and a couple of other things and offered them to me. What sensitivity, what spontaneous kindness. How could I refuse? If only I'd been able then to tell him, *kimochi dake itadakimasu*, one of those untranslatable Japanese phrases that you say to avoid offending someone, something like "no thank you but I truly accept your good will." As soon as I accepted the food, he gave me his impeccable business card. I couldn't read it. He told me his name and that he was from the south. Speaking correct English, he asked me if he could help me with anything. I told him no. He looked worried. He knew that something terrible was happening to me. I couldn't look him in the eye. Silence and more silence.

The train arrived at Nagoya. Kyoto was the next station. I felt that I should give him an explanation before arriving at my destination but I began to see the Kyoto Tower in the distance and, unexpectedly, pagodas and more pagodas. Anyway, Don Toño, my father's friend, was to blame for having given him those postcards of Kyoto. As a girl, I used to spend hours lost among those eaves and rosettes, on the balustrades of those pagodas. I'd invested so many illusions onto those postcards, now gnawed away by time, that it wasn't fair for me to keep crying. I got up from my seat and thanked the passenger with a bow. I said goodbye and later I remembered that I'd hadn't even told him my name or where I was from.

That visit I stayed in Kyoto only a week. The beauty of its temples and gardens made me feel the same serenity as when we used to get up early and go for walks in Chapultepec Park. In Kyoto I noticed the contrasts between the traditional and the modern. Aside from the temples, many of the typical houses were made completely of wood. Time had stood still there. But there were also new buildings and anywhere you looked, there were vending machines that sold milk, coffee, hot soup, magazines, beer and even condoms. In Mexico City this didn't exist; there were only machines that dispensed bitter, horrible coffee. I walked a few times along the Kamo River. What a delight! Why weren't there rivers in my city? Then I understood my obsession of going for endless walks around the new lake in Chapultepec. I left Kyoto without knowing that destiny would impel me to return there again and again.

I arrived in Hirakata Shi, a city to the northeast of Osaka province. Friends I'd known in Mexico City were waiting for me there. I went to live with them in the apartments surrounding the university campus. That's when I learned what it meant to live in a small space. As a child I never got tired of watching the TV program *Señorita Cometa* and I knew very well just how small the Japanese living space was: the living room is dining room and bedroom at the same time. And OK, that wasn't so bad as not having a place to bathe. You had to go to the *sento*, that is, to the public baths at night. Alright, it wasn't necessary to bathe at night but that's how they did it so I did too. I was lucky that my first time, my friend Higa Setsuko went with me. She was a really cool girl who was hardly a student but who already spoke Spanish almost perfectly. The baths were divided into a section for men and another for women. You had to carry a tray with your shampoo and soap. They didn't use sponges but a nylon washcloth one foot long and six inches wide. When you entered the baths, you paid and then went into the dressing rooms. You had to undress in front of all the other women and place your clothes and towel in an individual compartment. A sliding door led to the immense bath. To the left and right there were faucets fifteen inches high. Above each faucet, a decent-sized mirror; and in front there was a little plastic bench. We sat down there, shoulder to shoulder, the same way God brought us into the world. We turned on the hot and cold faucets. The water fell onto the tray and that's how we bathed, like someone who pours water, little by little, over her head with a gourd. I felt embarrassed that my body looked so different from the other women's. I had more of a butt, a bigger bust and, above all, more of a belly. They were much whiter than I was and their skin was like a baby's. Although I wasn't even twenty, there were already signs of stretch-marks on my body. I felt uncomfortable. Being so different gave me an inferiority complex. With time I got used to the pools of boiling water where the others entered after bathing but I never felt good being naked in front of them. But alright, that's another story.

The worst wasn't the public bath where I went to bathe but the bathrooms where you answered nature's call. Just imagine. When you enter the restroom at some station or other public place, to your right or left are the sinks with their individual mirrors or a long mirror. In front of the mirror and sinks are the individual stalls with their respective doors. You enter. You turn. You close the door. You hang your purse if there is a place to hang it. You pull down your underwear. You sit watching the door and then you have to suffer the torture of reading all the horrible graffiti that people have scribbled there. At first, in Japan I used the same places as everyone else except that many of the toilets weren't the familiar pots but long receptacles at floor level. So, you had to do your business quickly, just like when you went to small towns in Mexico and found yourself in an outhouse that only had a wooden hole.

In Japan the bathrooms were ultra-modern, made of stone, but the concept was the same. What I didn't understand until much later was that those bathrooms were designed for people to sit crouching but facing the wall and not the door like we're used to doing. I don't want to be disrespectful so it's better not to go into more details. I only want to say that my ignorance made me splash everything in the wrong direction. What a shame. The whole thing was a complete disaster. And in Japanese houses there are special sandals for the bathroom. When you enter, you're supposed to take off your sandals, leave them outside, and use the ones that are inside, set there, ready to be worn. If you make the mistake of not using the sandals that are exclusively for the bathroom and just enter without leaving your own outside, no one will know that you're inside and can open the door and catch you with your pants down. Most Japanese doors were made of wood and didn't have locks so that making innocent mistakes could result in a catastrophe. I learned by making mistakes and looking ridiculous but I guess that it's never too late to learn.

At first I was always hungry. It wasn't so much that I missed *chiles*, beans, and tortillas but that the portions looked small to me. I ate the dishes with the most food: croquettes, breaded pork or fish, and everything that was plentiful. The typical Japanese meal fascinated me from the beginning but since my appetite was such that I was capable of eating two small plates of food, I just couldn't afford it. Going to the supermarket and trying to cook was worse because I only knew how to cook with garlic, onions, *chiles*, and other things that I couldn't find. Let's say that Hirakata Shi was a small town but its supermarkets were ultra-modern, with automatic doors and everything beautifully presented. To begin with, I came from another part of the world where supermarkets and shops were a fiesta of abundance. In Japan it wasn't so much the shortages as the uncanniness sensed by my eyes, which were used to profusion. I soon learned that in Japan everything revolves around specific seasons; everything changes, even the colors and flavors. In Mexico I only knew that when one began to see *jícamas*, limes, guavas, and *tejocotes*, Christmas was coming. It was already June and I was surprised that there was air-conditioning in the supermarkets but not in my apartment. A sultry humid heat, tropical style, was seeping into my very depths.

One day I ventured to Osaka. I left without taking an umbrella. I was wearing denim pants and suede shoes. It was very uncomfortable in that infernal humidity but I had little summer clothing and no decent sandals to wear outdoors. On my way back, I was caught in a downpour and got on the train soaking wet. People devoured me with their stares. I soon learned that it was imperative to listen to the weather report to be prepared for outdoors. What did I know about this since in Mexico it rains from May to September, it's never that hot and as far as umbrellas go. . . they're often more trouble than they're worth. I wish the earth could swallow me up, I said to myself. From that day onward I always I felt embarrassment and stress; yes, incredible stress. Because of the way I looked, the Japanese almost never realized that I was a foreigner and on a day like that they thought I was crazy.

I got off the train still possessed by those stares. It was suffocating to walk in that humidity and the constant drizzle. It had only rained on us like that one day in Acapulco. But, who cared! We were on vacation at the beach! Still stunned by memories of Acapulco Bay, as I left the station, I walked right instead of left. I was lost. I thought that I'd find my way immediately but no. Suddenly a little old woman seventy years old approached and covered me with her navy-blue umbrella. She asked me where I was going. That way, I told her, close to the university. She asked me a couple of other questions and then we didn't speak. We approached the station and I thought that she'd leave me there but no; she insisted on taking me to my destination. The Japanese never cease to surprise me with their courtesy. What could that little old hunchbacked woman have been thinking along the way, she who could barely walk but did? Such kindness amazed me more and more and even made me feel uncomfortable; how could I return that huge favor? I'd only had that same sensation when we used to go to the Tiradores Hacienda in Michoacán. The people on the ranch there gave us their turkeys as we took leave of them, even knowing that they might go without eating for a day. By the time we arrived at the dormitory, the rain had almost erased those intense stares I'd felt on the train. Then the worst thought occurred to me, how could I thank her for her infinite kindness? When we arrived at my apartment, a powerful feeling was tearing out my soul; I wanted to shout out *gracias*, thank you, from the bottom of my heart, thank you for your courtesy. But not understanding why, the only thing that came out of my mouth was saying *thank you* two times, I lowered my gaze and offered her a bow. Far from feeling happy at having returned home, I felt as if my tongue had been cut out. I was puzzled because I'd meant to do something more. I felt at a loss, empty.

With time I learned that in Japanese a couple of words are enough. I also learned that one should speak little because talking too much is considered bad manners. I learned all that and I followed the rules with a saint's devotion. I also learned that in a conversation one must allow pauses, silence, and more silence. Without realizing it, I began to imitate their expressions, to avoid grimacing and gesturing or speaking with my hands the way I do when I become emotional in my own language. All that made me see myself as more and more Japanese. When I observed other foreigners who lived in Japan, they even made me feel envious because, unlike them, I could not be myself. They continued speaking with the same inflections of their languages, with the same manners, wearing the same strange clothes. They hadn't changed as much as I had.

One day I heard someone say that we Mexicans get along well with the Japanese because we're both submissive peoples. That hurt me but at the time, I wasn't used to taking such things seriously. I only knew that I felt good imitating the tone of their voice and everything they did. I don't know how much time passed since I'd met the passenger on the train and the old lady who accompanied me in the rain, but one day I came to the conclusion that my few words, my silence and my sincere bows had been enough thanks for them. When I met them I wanted to tell them *thank you* from the bottom of my heart but at that time I didn't know how to say "heart." In Japanese, the word "heart" is *kokoro* and the sound of the word is charming but it's never used as it is in Spanish. The word *yasashii* describes the spirit and goodness of the Japanese people. I remember that when I took classes in calligraphy, one day the instructor brought in a brush twenty inches long and orange ink. He offered to write what we asked him to, a poem or a character, on large pieces of paper that looked like parchment. Please write *kokoro yasashii*, I told him. He looked at me, surprised; he couldn't believe it. For me, that was the spirit of a people who'd opened the doors of my new home, of my new language.

Two years later, back in Mexico, I sent the passenger a Christmas card, one of those tacky ones I'd bought tons of in the Santo Domingo Plaza and that I liked at the time. In a note using my best Japanese, I told him I thought of him now and then and that I'd cried that day because I couldn't believe destiny had finally called on me to know Kyoto. I never imagined that when things are too good to be true they cause pain and weeping. And so, out of pure embarrassment, I didn't dare tell him what had happened to me that day. I received a response from him. He wrote just one line: "I am sure that you enjoyed Japan but there is no place like home." I never heard from him again. He was right but only to a certain point . . . one year later I was already back in Japan. I'd found my own home there as well.

Araceli in Kyoto, 1981.

Kyoto, 1981.

Arubaito
(Part-Time Work)

"You could be a prostitute."

"What do you mean, a prostitute? You've got to be kidding."

"Here prostitutes aren't prostitutes."

"Well, are they or aren't they?"

"OK, you could work in one of those *hostess clubs* or *snack bars*. The only thing you'd have to do there is serve customers their drinks, nothing else."

"But I'm not pretty or skinny."

"That doesn't matter, it's enough that you're a foreigner."

"Hmmm."

"Or in the worst case, you could get into women's wrestling. The only problem is you have to come out naked. Well, naked but covered with mud so that no one sees anything. The only tricky part is wrestling in the mud. That's all. They pay you a lot of money for fighting just a little while."

"Me? Naked? Covered with mud doing a show? Not if I were crazy!"

Those were the conversations I had with the pals I'd met in Mexico who were learning Spanish. All those conversations began a month after my arrival in Japan, when I was thinking of staying longer but frankly didn't know how.

Arubaito means working half-time or part-time. Later I discovered that *arubaito* wasn't Japanese but one of countless foreign words used in Japan. *Arubaito* comes from German and means *arbeit*, which is work but not part-time work, as it's used in Japan. Well, I don't want to complicate things, just to say that it really surprised me that so many high-school and university students had an *arubaito*.

They worked as dishwashers, busboys, waiters and waitresses, packers, salespeople, cashiers, and anything else you can imagine. Put another way, these young people were the Japanese jacks-of-all-trades. But to have an *arubaito* was a respectable thing because it meant that one didn't have a steady job and that he or she only worked a certain number of hours. At that time in Mexico, those types of jobs were full-time and all kinds of people did them. They weren't part-time jobs for students. In Japan I was surprised by the professionalism and dignity with which *arubaitos* were performed. It's not to say that in Mexico things weren't done like that. No sir. Nobody teaches a Mexican to work hard. He or she is simply a good worker. As if it were already in our blood. It's enough to see a ten-year-old boy packing bags in a grocery store to realize that Mexican children are as professional as those young Japanese. The only difference is that in Mexico at that time, students weren't recruited to do those possibly undesirable tasks while in Japan it was normal to do so. So, in that country, owners of restaurants or gasoline stations, stores, and even companies right and left were recruiting for *arubaitos* so that students could work without receiving loans. They were paid by the hour and that was it.

I wasn't interested in what the Japanese call *mizu shōbai*, which means *the water trade*. Don't get scared, it has absolutely nothing to do with either swimming or with selling canisters of water. It's more about everything related to night-time entertainment, nightclubs, the famous *hostess clubs* or *snack bars*, everything that has to do with booze and absolute ruin. The world of *the water trade* wasn't a secret. Everyone knew about it and spent time gossiping about it. In the *hostess clubs* they recruited women and if they were foreigners, even better. They were the ones who waited on the customers. Waiting on them meant basically serving them drinks and entertaining them with good conversation. Apparently that was all. The so-called *snack bars* were the same except that the drinks were ridiculously expensive. Yes, of course, they served the customers a *snack*, but a *snack* at what price? They hooked them when they made them buy a super-expensive bottle of whiskey. And if the customer couldn't finish the bottle, he'd sign his name on the label, and they'd hold it for him until he returned. That's how they kept the clients happy, since they returned again and again to the same place. The *snack bars* weren't exclusively for men because sometimes they brought their partners. On the other hand, almost all the bartenders were women, often impeccably dressed in kimonos with beautifully coiffed hair.

Thousands of foreigners went to Japan just for that, to work in *the water trade*. At that time, the ones who came from Latin America were mostly Brazilians and Colombians. From Asia came Philippine, Indonesian, and Thai women. It was said that they earned a fortune. Some were runaways or they did it out of pure necessity, working in something that was even harder: in what they call *fūzoku*, or the sex industry, which is made up of *sōpurando, pincusaron, fashon jerusu* and *imeikura*. Just a minute. Don't despair. I didn't understand it at first, either. Later I learned that in English this meant nothing less than *Soap Land, Pink Salon, Fashion Health* and *Image Club*, although for me those names didn't mean anything in one language or another. They said that those so-called *sōpurando* were like brothels. Those pick-up places also functioned as baths where the customers were cleaned — out, that is; that was the origin of the words *soap* (*sōpu*) and *land* (*rando*), or *paradise*. Massages were also provided there, and later, barter exchanges. It was said that the *pincusaron* or pink salons had nothing pink about them. Their specialty was nothing less than oral sex. The client went there for that. They say that in one huge room there were various cabins or compartments where the customer entered, was offered something to drink and immediately afterwards, *how do you do*. . . . Also practiced there was something called *sumata* (yes, that's a Japanese word), which they say means sex without penetration. Whoever wants to know more about this subject can look it up (the Japanese give Japanese names to the strangest things).

Now let's get serious. According to Japanese law, it's illegal to charge money for making love. Or maybe it's forbidden to prostitute oneself, but between word and action, there's plenty of wiggle-room. Let's continue. The *fashon jeresu* or *fashion health* have nothing to do with fashion or health. Well, let the men who frequent those places confirm that. They're nightclubs where massages are provided and every kind of activity takes place. Everything except making love because the law apparently prohibits it. And finally, the tackiest and silliest name I ever heard: *imeikura*. They say that women there disguise themselves grotesquely as nurses, secretaries, or whatever, and act like they're in a play as they perform erotic acts. I don't know if that's the truth or a lie, but I heard it over and over.

Since I wasn't born for either *the water trade* or the sex industry or, even less so, had the need for either, I asked the mother of a friend who was very rich, to be sure, to give me an *arubaito* of whatever kind she could. She received me in her opulent, typically Japanese house surrounded by a beautiful garden. Inside it was spacious, cold and

21

sad. At that time I didn't understand Japanese décor, which to my eyes seemed made up of opaque colors and immense spaces. Whole rooms without a single piece of furniture, planks of wood without a single nail.

"You can work in the house where you're living. All you have to do is cut cloth. It's easy. I'll pay you by how many yards you cut. That's it."

In effect, she gave me yards and yards of finely-woven cashmere cloth. I had to cut the thread at the ends and make a kind of fringe or frayed edge. It was lonely, boring work. The torrid summer heat made my days interminable. Since it was piece-work and I wasn't paid by the hour, what I liked to do was quickly use up all the rolls of cloth. I put the rolled-up cloth on the table and little by little went about making the fringe. I almost never felt comfortable working at Japanese tables because I had to kneel over the mat and my legs would fall asleep up to the knee. The house I lived in was dark. In fact, in order to save money, the lights weren't turned on. Air conditioning? Not in my dreams. And to top it off, every now and then a train passed by in back and the house shook. I felt as if the house were on the tracks and that at any moment a loose car would destroy us. I imagined the worst and kept cutting. Then I nostalgically remembered the summers in my city. The reds, whites, oranges, and yellows of its houses. The resplendent sun and the dry heat. The rain at twilight and that fresh, delicate air. But as I was seated at that table, the humidity made me sweat and so it wouldn't drip on the cloth, I wrapped a little white towel around my throat to prevent myself from rubbing it every now and then. This custom of wrapping a towel around your throat during physical labor is very Japanese. I also became aware that during the sultry summer heat, people used a little towel instead of a handkerchief. It was a strange custom but there I was, doing the same thing.

Of course the lady, whose last name was Karia, soon realized that I didn't like the work. It was one of two things: either I worked too slowly or I did it badly, I suppose. So she asked me if I wanted to work in one of her restaurants and I immediately told her *yes*. The truth is I'd never been a waitress or anything like that but feeling emboldened, I accepted her offer. To my great surprise, her restaurant was in the country, in the Gifu province, right in the midst of the rice-fields. It was a *rāmen* shop. Yes, in effect, all that was sold there was noodle-soup. I imagined that I was in Mexico:

"Give me one with tripe."

"One with trotters for me."

"Just throw in a few gizzards."

"Some necks and feet in mine."

And me with my Japanese still so rough, I barely understood what they were saying to me. The customers were workers who also wore white towels but across their foreheads. They dressed in white undershirts and black trousers that were baggy as far as the knee, and fitted from knee to ankle. At noon they took a lunch-break and went for their hot soup in the middle of that suffocating, sweltering heat. I remembered people from Veracruz and Guerrero eating fish and crab soup out in the sun. *Rāmen*, of course, is one of the cheapest and most filling dishes.

The restaurant had a rectangular-shaped bar. Thank God! If it had been any other shape, I wouldn't have known how to properly carry a tray with an enormous bowl of soup. And asking the customer what I could offer him was even worse. Three of us worked at the bar, a good reason why I never found myself in a tight spot. I helped by giving the customer *oshibori*, a small damp towel, white and cold, because it was summer. With that he'd clean his hands and even his face. Then I gave him *mugicha*, roasted barley iced tea. I also helped serve soup. So there I was in the middle of the rice-fields serving Japanese country people. It only occurred to me as I lived through these experiences that although they weren't necessary, they taught me a lot about life. After a while, I got bored. I simply never felt comfortable in the country.

At that time, Karia-kun, the woman's son, asked me, "why don't you go to the city of Nagoya? I know people there who could offer you more interesting work." Karia-kun spoke impeccable Spanish. He'd studied in Seville and had lived awhile in Mexico. Nagoya is located an hour from Gifu and, since it was a city, there were more opportunities there than in the country. So I decided to go there to introduce myself to Karia-kun's acquaintances.

My arrival in Nagoya changed the direction of my life over the next four years and marked me forever. But that's another story and it's very long, so I'll leave it for later. In Nagoya, I had some *arubaitos* that were amusing. A millionaire, owner of a gas-station (in Japan, gas stations are privately owned) and good friends with Kimiko—the woman who became my protector when I arrived—asked me to be his "aide-de-camp" during the opening of his new gasoline station. My job consisted of standing outside with a flag as if I were at a drag race. That way I could attract passing cars to buy gas. The truth is it embarrassed me doing that kind of work. On the other hand, they paid me well so it was a temptation I couldn't resist or reject. I also ended up modeling for the famous architect Hayakawa Fumihiko. He did an oil painting of me that I rescued from his house after his death and that I still treasure.

On several occasions, I got a more sophisticated kind of *arubaito*. I was asked to be a "cultural attaché." It came from Dentsu, the biggest advertising agency in Japan and the whole world. The staff-people waited for me in the reception area and treated me as if I were made of velvet, with a kindness and graciousness that made me feel important. Then they started asking me questions that were so strange and simple, like:

"In your opinion, what is the most interesting thing about Oaxaca?"

"What type of clothing should one wear when traveling from Mexico City to Cuernavaca?"

"How many times have you visited the Anthropology Museum?"

Or, even better, they made me correct short phrases, like:

"Life is an excursion."

"Sensational flavor."

"Spice of the day."

Several days had to pass for me to realize that my humble role as attaché was gold for them. Like good publicists, they were working on advertisements for Latin America. Their consultations lasted a few minutes and they paid me what generally took me three days to earn. That type of work was very lucrative because the Japanese valued highly whomever could teach them things. Because of that, knowing English or being an English teacher at the beginning of the '80s meant real luxury, status, a good salary, bonuses. . . .

On occasion, professional interpreters also requested my services. They asked me questions that seemed basic and not at all complicated but since it was a professional consultation, they received me with honors. They offered me tea or coffee. They sat me down and began questioning me little by little with those satiny voices of Japanese women. I never felt so important. Those interpreters were graduates of the largest universities in Tokyo, Waseda, Sofia and, above all, Nanzan, one of the biggest Catholic universities, located right in Nagoya. Teaching Spanish there was more important than teaching French, and almost as important as teaching English. It was a very prestigious institution. After the consultation, they offered me cake or chocolates and they paid me, oh how they paid me! I fondly remember Teranishi Takako, one of the country's most brilliant and important interpreters. She always treated me well, she always respected me and made me feel that my world and my language were worthy things.

I also began giving informal classes in Spanish conversation. I used to meet with a group of studious and engaged people. Some had learned the language on their own and spoke a half-cockeyed and affected Spanish. Others had learned the grammar well at school but weren't fluent. And a couple of them were, as a radio station in Mexico says, fans of *ranchera* music. They knew the words to a countless number of songs, backwards and forwards, they had *charro* suits and learned the lyrics by heart so they could memorize and practice our music, which they adored. They didn't pay me as much as the interpreters did but they were very grateful and we always went out to dinner after class. It was almost incongruous to find such enthusiasm for my language and culture in that remote corner of the world.

I had various *arubaitos*, as many as possible, and I always did my work responsibly. I was always grateful for the opportunities people gave me. This taught me a lot about Japan and I learned to value my language and culture like never before. After I left Japan, the *arubaitos* expanded greatly. Something they call "seasonal work" was also revived, something that had been banned for decades. For me, it's the same song with a different tune because seasonal work is destined for those who work every day and go from contract to contract and thus continue working without benefits for years on end. The *arubaito* wasn't exactly a form of exploitation but surely a way of generating more profits while contracting good, cheap labor. Seasonal work was and still is done almost completely by women, most of them married, who work in agriculture, sales, or in offices.

It never crossed my mind to become a *hostess* in a *club*, much less to work in a *snack bar*. I had what I needed with the *arubaitos*. Through them I came to know the Japanese better. They also learned from me.

Working at the gas station,
1982.

Working at a stand outside the grounds of the Nagoya Castle,
1984.

Eru Chipo
(*"El Tipo"*)

She always arrived just bathed and happy. With the joy of women in love who are pleased by everything. He was always dressed in a suit with his hair nicely combed. She was coquettish, tall, slender, with shoulder-length curly hair and scarlet lipstick. She always wore brightly-colored, well-fitting clothes, high heels and net stockings. They went out to dinner every Wednesday at seven in the evening. They sat at table number four, the one in the corner with two rattan-and-bamboo seats facing the wall so that no one could see their faces. They always ordered the seafood casserole, the most expensive dish, which included lobster and a variety of gourmet fish. They drank a bottle of Rioja although sometimes, on a whim, they changed for a German Riesling. Sometimes they began with Serrano ham, sausage, squid and then their casserole, and on occasion they ordered a *paella valenciana*. From a distance, it was clear that they were lovers or at least that's what we thought. A typical couple never ate with such hunger or with such passion. Or never arrived looking so contented. We never learned their names. Back then no one paid by credit card. It was an embarrassment to do so because it was a sign that the person didn't have money and needed advance credit. People always paid, as much as possible, with crisp new bills. They would take out two or three 10,000-yen notes although it might only be to use one of them. The important thing was to show that they were carrying enough cash.

      The brand of their wallets was very important. They were almost always imported from France, Italy, or were some Japanese brand then in vogue. They were made and finished in the most sophisticated hides of astrakhan, zebra, vicuña, and I don't know what else. The woman's lover never asked for a receipt, not so much because it might have been a disgrace if his wife found out. No. Asking for a receipt would look very bad. It was only done when a company was going to cover the expense and that was that. For this reason, almost everything was handled in cash. I soon learned to receive money as it was done there. We had a little rectangular tray where we'd put the check and present it to the customer so he or she could read it. I learned the art of give-and-take there. Giving and receiving had to be done with delicacy, as if you were performing a graceful dance comparable to a ballet. Both hands were always used and, as much as possible, objects, in this case the tray, had to rest on your palms. We received money the same way. On one side of the cash register we had an abacus to add up charges. How ironic that we didn't have a calculator in the very country where so many were produced. It was assumed that in Japan, everyone had learned to use an abacus since childhood, either in math class or in specialized schools. But in the end, being slow, I never learned it very well and it embarrassed me to use it. I trembled when it came time to make change. Let's say that the total was 15,350 yen and someone paid with 20,000 yen. It was assumed that the server would have to subtract mentally and give exact change: "your change is 4,650 yen." And when the matter was very complicated, the server would use the abacus but it was taken for granted that he or she was good at math. The change was also put on the tray with the bills well arranged, face-up, with the denomination facing the customer.

There were other unlikely couples. The men were fat and old or had faces like alcoholics. The women were young and always well-dressed but had bad taste. They lacked poise. Their voices were as shallow as their gestures and when they ate, they did so more out of obligation than desire. It was curious because in general women in love eat little. The spark of love takes away hunger. But in these cases, everything was reversed. We supposed that these were those lovers who did everything out of necessity. One Sunday, one of those old, fat men came in, desperate, slamming the door, and almost shouting, said, "I'm bringing in my family. I hope it doesn't occur to you all to talk about me." As if we were stupid . . . as if we'd been born yesterday. But not all of them were old *sukebe*. Dirty old men. TV people, doctors, lawyers, dentists, professors, musicians and artists also used to spend time there. In the end, a group of incredibly interesting characters. We even ended up dining with Narciso Yepes, whom we'd invited to the restaurant after his debut. Years later, according to what my friends told me, Paco de Lucía, the Gipsy Kings and other famous groups also came there.

The Japanese are very open people. They love to taste new things. They were always anxious to try different dishes, to drink wines they'd never imagined. My own family was always like that and I suppose because of that, I felt at home in Japan. Foreigners also came to the restaurant, although very few of them. It was fun to talk with them, when possible; I should say, whenever they spoke in Spanish or Japanese. Once a couple came in. He was blonde with blue eyes. She was, too. She looked like a doll. After reading and rereading the menu, which of course was in Spanish and Japanese, they began asking me questions. Since I didn't understand a word of what they were saying to me, I asked them in the most awkward English I've ever pronounced in my life, *Do you speak English*? I'll never forget the expression on their faces. They were British and they'd asked me very rapidly where the lamb was imported from but since I didn't understand that expression or their accent, I did the most ridiculous thing I'd ever done. Afterwards, they realized I didn't have bad intentions and began to come often to the restaurant.

Foreigners and clever, brilliant Japanese worked in the restaurant. Everyone spoke Spanish or English and had lived outside the country. It was the first and most authentic Spanish restaurant in Nagoya. It was a white house designed in a Mediterranean style with various levels. The entrance was an archway leading to a staircase, with flowerpots on the left and right. The door to the lobby was rustic, Spanish-style with shutters and grillwork; it was hand-carved, made of solid pine with forged iron nails and fittings. As customers passed through that door, time transported them to another place. It was like being in Spain. All the furniture was also rustic. It had been bought in Castile and Andalusia. There were glass cabinets, tables, cupboards, sideboards, arches, armoires, shelves, wrought-iron tables with glazed tiles, mirrors and even bulls' heads. The dishes were made of Andalusian ceramic in blue, green, and yellow hues. The table-cloths were hand-made lace, embroidered by an old-fashioned sewing machine or, even better, cross-stitched. Only cassettes of Spanish music were played. Every kind was included, flamenco, classical guitar and singers like Rafael, Rocío Durcal, and Julio Iglesias. The food was authentic and was prepared by Spaniards and Japanese chefs whose training had been in Spain, the latter guaranteed to serve dishes with a Japanese touch.

Since there was money to burn, the *Eru Chipo* (*El Tipo*) restaurant, a name that Ei-Chan, Kimiko's brother-in-law, gave it, was always filled with people. For a meal and a bottle of wine for two, a customer paid up to 15,000 yen (approximately 150 U.S. dollars) and there were some who came in two or three times a week. When December arrived, there wasn't enough room in the place because groups would come to celebrate Christmas and New Year's Eve. I decided to work in *El Tipo* because the owner offered me a salary much higher than what the Japanese were receiving. Actually it wasn't fair for me to earn more than they did but the owner thought that I deserved more because I spoke Spanish. The truth is that it wasn't necessary to speak in Spanish with anyone but it was seen as something prestigious. There were also a couple of Spanish women who switched schedules. Like me, they were well-paid but they fought often. Carmen was Catalonian, and Pepita, Andalusian. But between the two of them, they never stopped complaining. I got along well with both of them. In fact, it amused me because I was learning a lot. I got tired of hearing about the best restaurants on the Ramblas, about Montaña de Montjuic, about the Sagrada Familia, about the streets and constructions of Barrio Gótico and about Miró and Gaudí. Pepita wasn't an educated woman and had been born in some forgotten town. She didn't have much to show off but she did have a sharp tongue. No foreigner could match her. She knew it and had so much self-confidence that she even began working on TV. To infuriate Carmen, in a moment of rage, Pepita went to live in Barcelona where she started her own travel agency and bought a luxury condo. For my part I always kept my mouth shut and did my work.

It wasn't worth going to work in another area, above all because I wanted to stay in Japan for only a few months. If my job was only an *arubaito* at best, even though I worked almost forty hours a week, my salary was amazing and I was well liked by everyone. I don't know if it was something mysterious but I always worked well with Japanese people. Arriving late for work was unforgiveable, above all because the buses and the subway ran on a strict schedule; so I never came in late. Everything, absolutely everything, had to do with working as a team; individualism wasn't allowed. Since in Japan the custom of leaving a tip doesn't exist, we all earned a very decent salary and our only objective was to treat the customers well. It was a very expensive family restaurant in spite of the good and bad couples who came into the place. So I worked in a friendly and secure atmosphere. There was no cashier or waiter or busboy or bartender or janitor there. We all had to do every task and everything was done in a group. We always helped each other out. It was taken for granted that we had to be respectful and friendly with our co-workers and especially with the customers. We all served the same tables, we all went out of our way to offer impeccable service. Finally, *okyakusama wa kamisama desu*. The customer is God. That was the motto of all Japanese business.

For me, it was very easy to work in that environment because there wasn't any confrontation or favoritism. I was always a real fighter and competitive and although I never caused any problems, it was clear that I liked to stand out.

"Tomorrow is our day off, what do you want to do?"

"I'm coming in to spruce up the restaurant. A few things need to be cleaned and put in order."

"But tomorrow is our day off and the restaurant is closed . . . "

"I don't care. What am I going to do with so many free hours in a day? I prefer to come in to work."

When I began with that attitude, it was clear that I was going against the group and since it had to do with work, everyone felt obliged to help me. So all of us ended up not having a day off every time I felt like coming in. All the full-time staff earned a fixed salary but I didn't. They paid me by the hour, like in an *arubaito*, but since it had been my idea to go into work on a day off, I wasn't paid for that day. It didn't bother me because I enjoyed taking on tasks. They also didn't pay any over-time. So, I was an individualist who'd forced my co-workers to do what at bottom they didn't want to do. At the time I never thought that way but the truth is that I've always been obsessed with work.

For some reason, on Thursdays, when the restaurant was closed, it used to rain all day. I wasn't used to seeing such sad, stormy days from morning to night. I began to have unbearable headaches. At that time I didn't understand that they were allergies triggered by the humidity and the change in weather. There wasn't much I could do except go shopping or out to dinner in the neighborhood. I didn't go to the movies because I still didn't understand Japanese well enough and it was very expensive in those days. I became annoyed by the same routine. Because of that, one fine day when I didn't have anything to do, I said to the owner:

"You shouldn't close the restaurant on Thursdays. After all, your staff can take turns and rotate shifts. That way, they'll even be able to take off Saturdays or Sundays and not just Thursdays."

"No, I've always closed on Thursdays and I'm afraid that my customers might not come."

"How much do you want to bet? Try it out. Leave it open for one month and then you'll see that it will be filled.

Said and done. And of course, the owner was always delighted with my suggestions. I've always had business in my veins. My mother was raised by her uncle-and aunt, sour closed-minded hicks who only were worried about their profits. They didn't have children and didn't know what to do with their money. They sold livestock although they didn't raise them and their whole lives were dedicated to business. At home, they had a cook and a maid. Fun? For what? Sundays were enough for going out in a tailor-made dress, to show it off at church and then in the atrium outside.[1] Vacations? Once a year, to the city.

"Señor taxi-driver. Drive us around the city. We'll pay you by the hour, by the day, whatever you want. If I've got too much of anything, it's money. I wish I had enough time to spend it! The only reason I don't carry more is because I'm not a burro."

"Going to school? Why would anyone want to go to school if they could pay a teacher to come to the house? After all, here they give a girl a few lessons and that's plenty. This idea of leaving the house all the time to go to some school is dangerous. You learn from life and work, not from school. From work you learn how to count, to memorize, to battle people and those sons of b. . . ."

My mother grew up in that environment, like a poor rich girl who had everything except a formal education and that's what she longed for most. She also was obsessive, but about reading. When chance placed a book in her hands and she liked it, she read it in silence and then out loud once, twice, three, ten times. She memorized passages and complete stories, down to their periods and commas. I don't know if that practice trained her to remember the smallest details even when she was very old. But, when she was a girl, without realizing it, she learned from her uncle and aunt to work and live from work and for work and that was part of the education she instilled in me.

So there I found myself, spending my days with Japanese people, working as much or more than they did, trying to be and do the best I could. I wasn't a farm-worker or a wetback who'd crossed the Pacific out of necessity. I was one of so many Mexicans who lose their way out in the world. One of so many who barely leave a trace. I remember that years later I read a sentence by the author Ignacio Manuel Altamirano that taught me so much. He said something like this: "Mexicans never travel and when they do they never write."

---

1 An esplanade or square outside the church, with a kiosk in the center surrounded by benches, where couples and families socialize on Sunday after mass.

Why didn't I learn that lesson when I was in Japan? Why do I come to many things so early, and others, too late? As destiny is full of surprises, exactly between 1981 and 1982, Mexico suffered one of the most drastic economic crises of its history. Mexico, more than any other country, was appearing on the front pages of the most important newspapers. Since 1981, much was being said about the falling price of oil and about the increase in interest rates. To top it off, in 1982, our beloved President López Portillo suspended payments on the foreign debt, devalued the Mexican peso and, as his crowning glory, nationalized the banks and other key industries. Because of that, my father's business collapsed, and my brother, who had a good position in ICA[2], also lost his job; the business where all my cousins worked shut down too. All of a sudden, they were unemployed. Because of all this, my desire to return to Mexico diminished more and more.

Various families who went to the restaurant began to give me tips, not out of pity but because my service really stood out. I never spent that money by myself; with it I bought chocolates or a bottle of wine and shared them with my co-workers. That was another custom of theirs. You had to share with everyone. Sometimes it occurred to someone to bring in rice crackers and we all ate them. To show appreciation for the gesture, the next time someone else brought in fruit and the next, peanuts or some other item. When someone took a trip, he or she had to return with a gift from the place visited, what they call *omiyage*. This was an obligation, in fact. They would bring typical candies or pickled vegetables or various other specialties. Those customs had to be respected. The same thing happened when the owner felt like going somewhere after work. We were required to go with her and keep her company. Or if the crazy idea of going out dancing occurred to two in the group, all the others, whether we liked it or not, had to follow them. We had to show solidarity. In effect, my work companions became friends for life. I remember Maguchi Mihoko and Sako Hitomi with real affection. Both were exceptional workers and taught me everything with enormous patience. I also got on well with Ueda Akira, Hoshino Kazuya, Hayashi Yoji and Higashi Yasushi. The last two taught me about Spanish cooking and in their free moments gave me lessons in Japanese cuisine.

---

2 Ingenieros Civiles Asociados (Associated Civil Engineers), a prestigious infrastructure company.

After I'd worked a short time for Tezuka Kimiko, the owner of the place, she told me that I could come to live with her. She was a rich woman, well-traveled and she spoke Spanish and English quite well. She lived with her husband, Tezuka Toshimasa, whom we affectionately called Toshi-chan. He was a manager at Dentsu, the mega-advertising agency. They neither had nor wanted children. Work, money, and their belongings were the most important things to them. I never really understood why they were so friendly with me. To the point that, at first, I began thinking they were connected with the Mafia and wanted to kidnap me in order to sell me in some hidden corner of Asia. I wasn't being paranoid. You'd hear those monstrous stories so they must have been true. It terrified me that they might be mixed up in something horrific. But their conversations were normal. It seemed strange to me that they spoke so little but afterwards I realized that that's the way they were. In my ignorance, at first their speech seemed very frugal and spare to me. But in spite of everything, I accepted the offer to live with them because it was more convenient than traveling as far as Gifu every day. They lived in the penthouse of a new building next to the Central Park. Soon I practically became their daughter and their business confidante. Why did that woman have such confidence in me? I don't know. I never found out.

Araceli (center front) with co-workers at *El Tipo*; Tezuka Kimiko (right-front) and Maguchi Mihoko (left front), 1981.

Araceli (right) at *El Tipo* with Spanish classical guitarist Narciso Yepes;
Carmen Capdevila (left), 1984.

Yousai Gakkou
(Design School)

"Since you like art and fashion so much, I'm going to take you to a design school so you learn how to make your own clothes," Kimiko told me one morning when she saw me moping around. I'd never studied design or anything like it although I remember very well in junior high that the classes in dressmaking horrified me because as far as I could tell, they were classes for girls. No, I liked welding and book-binding. But since there were only boys in those workshops, I wasn't allowed to learn either of those trades. To my misfortune, I was forced to take shorthand and typing. The news knocked the wind out of me although much later I understood that one always learns something useful through repetition.

She took me to enroll in the Fuji Academy. It was right downtown, by Nishiki Street. At that time, my Japanese was very rudimentary and I was scared that I might not understand anything. The school was small; it basically took up the second floor of the building and on the main floor was a ladies' and gentleman's clothing boutique. We were assisted by Riu Tamiko, the teacher, a woman about 50 years old, nicely made up, her hair combed to the side in a full wave, like those styles from the sixties. She wore a fuschia-colored suit, almost Mexican pink, and black patent-leather high heels. I asked her if she'd made her suit and she told me yes, that she'd made all her clothes since she was fourteen.

"You'll start first thing tomorrow."

"But I don't have material or . . ."

"That doesn't matter, all you need is a pencil."

"A pencil?"

"Yes."

The classes ran Monday to Friday from ten in the morning to two in the afternoon. It was actually a lot of time but I never bothered thinking about those things.

I arrived looking very presentable and trembling, like a child eager to arrive on her first day of school. On the way to the academy I was thinking about my childhood, about those wonderful days when we'd begin school. The September rains at twilight left a peculiar smell in the gardens. The sun rose and the air smelled of wet earth. I loved to see the flowers and their leaves throbbing with that crystalline dew. The first day was always easy, without any school supplies or books to carry. That's how I felt that time, so light and inspired to learn that I took long strides without noticing. I carried a thin Kokuyo-brand notebook. It seemed obvious for me to have it although it may not have been required. As I arrived, the students were anxiously waiting for me; they'd already heard that a foreigner was about to start class. It was Wednesday, right in the middle of the week and almost the end of September. For me, it was a very strange week because in Mexico classes always started on the second day of September, after the State of the Nation address, and I don't know why but I believed that they should have started on a Monday, not a Wednesday.

The teacher introduced me to my classmates. Most of them were between twenty and twenty-four years old. Only two were married and there were three more mature women. I didn't feel strange although all of them were older than I was. They received me enthusiastically and, as the morning passed, they rained more and more questions down on me. Conversation classes? What good would those do if I had to talk like a chatterbox there? From my classmates I learned gestures and manners, intonations, refrains, and exquisite phrases used only by women. I who'd so despised classes just for girls felt loved and respected there.

The first day I began to trace a basic dress pattern because it was the easiest thing to do. My teacher gave me the material. Later little by little she ordered me a measuring tape, tracing paper, scissors for paper and fabric, a glue-stick, pins, a chalk-wheel marker and a couple of other things. When I went to buy fabric at the Chikusa station, my eyes couldn't believe it: there were pre-cut dresses; the only thing you had to do was the fittings. But even with that, first we had to trace it on paper to be sure that the garment came out right. Instead of spending weeks explaining to me about tracing and measuring, my teacher put my hands to work on the spot. She taught me to use the electric sewing machine. At first I couldn't coordinate my hands with my right foot on the pedal. I became nervous and couldn't stop pedaling. As usual, my hands also couldn't stop and out of nervousness I pointed the fabric in different directions. That ended up a total disaster. She never criticized me for being all thumbs. On the contrary, she helped me unstitch that tangled labyrinth that had been left on the cloth. But more than cutting and design, at that school I learned how to function as part of Japanese society.

Without making lists or schedules, everyone took turns bringing in bread, sweets, chocolates, *onigiri*. On Mondays, someone arrived with *obanyaki*, freshly baked bread filled with sweet beans. Yes, that's what I just said: sweet beans. Please don't tell me that it disgusts you. I remember that one day a Japanese friend in Mexico told me that rice pudding made him nauseous because it was prepared with milk and sugar. I never understood until I was faced with bread filled with sweet black beans. But "when in Rome. . . ." Then someone brought out Japanese sweets. More than the flavor, the wrapping and design were a delight to our eyes. They came in a box and each one was wrapped carefully in what looked like rice paper. It felt like *Alice in Wonderland*; the box was a multicolored splendor. I didn't want to unwrap them because I was afraid that the magic might escape. Sometimes they were sweets made from a soft dough of rice, soy, or bean flour. On other occasions, inside was *mitarashi dango*, a brochette of little rice balls roasted with honey and pinches of salt. In the sitting-room there was tea to help us settle our stomachs when we overdid it and ate too much. Every once in a while, without planning it, two or three of us brought in several things at the same time. And there we were, talking, eating, designing, sewing, laughing. It was a good life, without suffering, without pain or problems to worry about. OK, I take it back. Every once in a while they talked about problems but those had to do with marriage.

Some of them didn't have a boyfriend and had already turned twenty-four. It was commonly accepted that a woman had to get married before she was 25 years old. Otherwise, she'd become an "old maid," a left-over. And not only that but women were told that they'd look like a "Christmas pastry on the 25th of December." That heavy and rotten expression meant that if a woman reached twenty-five and still was single, her value was automatically cut in half, like pastries and merchandise for Christmas that after Christmas Eve are offered at a cheap price. Practically for that reason alone they were going to design school. It was hoped that, at the very least, they might learn how to sew, embroider, and cook. They felt tremendous pressure because they desperately had to look for a boyfriend and be prepared for marriage at the same time. But they tried to hide their pain. They simply didn't show their worries. Instead of complaining, they kept quiet and did the almost-impossible to learn various things at once and they did everything very well with those artistic hands blessed by who knows what celestial being. After design school, they went to classes for flower-arranging, classes for the tea-ceremony, English classes, classes and more classes. Some also had an *arubaito* and worked a few hours.

From them I also learned how to share, how to work toward beginning each day in harmony, with a smile, with gentle words, with an offering. That custom of sharing things is very Japanese and at times even becomes an obligation but—and anyone who wants to challenge me is free to do so—who would be offended if he were offered something? Sometimes they would get up very early and cook a dish to take to school. A very simple item like *onigiri* or rice balls wrapped in seaweed and filled with *charal* fish or *chamoy*. So in that atmosphere I also taught myself how to cook. But putting that aside, I continued tracing and sewing. Little by little I learned about taking measurements, about sketches and the front- and rear-lines, adjustments, patterns, seams, and other important things. My designs were becoming more and more sophisticated: I made pleated skirts, tartan skirts and flared skirts. As far as dresses, I never made anything out of this world mostly because my teacher and classmates told me *stop!* no pleats at the waist, concentrate on simple or low-waisted designs. I always thanked them for that. They never told me directly but through their advice they hinted that I should avoid doing any fittings because I didn't have a waistline but did have a little belly. I even began making jackets from what looked like lambskin and other easier garments like pants or aprons. It would have been impossible to do all that without the help of my teacher. She took me by the hand, step by step and I understood all the points she made. I never felt inhibited. The Japanese have that gift of keeping an eye on you without making you feel small. Maybe for that reason, in work situations, Japanese people never become bosses without first being workers. They always know their job inside out and never pressure people to learn from dusk till dawn. They hold the belief that in order to arrive at the mountain's summit, you don't have to climb straight up, that it's better to meander along the path little by little. With that wisdom of thousands of years, my teacher watched me trace and sew. She was hopeful that I might learn well one day.

The rest of the students sewed beautiful garments: tweed and multi-piece skirts, suits, vests and even nightgowns. They learned much more quickly than I did, they designed better than I did, they darned better than I did. Why were they so adept? What did their hands have that mine didn't? I asked myself that same question years later when in a ceramics class, I passionately produced clay pots and, trying to outdo myself, I also tried to make abstract pieces. When I painted my pieces with a scarlet-red glaze like Indians used on their saris and put them in the kiln, all of them turned green and, to top it off, shattered. We finished the class and everyone had their pieces ready for the show. Mine were only shards of clay. What was there about me that when I tried to make something artistic, it always got ruined? But even with all that, in the design academy my imagination began to soar. I bought typical Japanese cloth, navy-blue cotton with geometric figures, and made three-quarter-length kimono-style blouses. My teacher and classmates explained to me that those designs had been inspired by the movement of waves and the structure of leaves on trees. The funny thing is that *yousai gakkou* means Western design school and I ended up making clothing that was almost Japanese.

As soon as they saw that I liked fabrics and Japanese models, they told me about different designs printed with dots, stripes and flowers. They taught me to distinguish between designs inspired by the landscape tradition in Japanese art and those that represented cranes, carp, tigers, owls, and their different meanings. I hadn't realized that there were some fabrics printed with figures of Japanese girls and women dressed in kimonos. They also taught me about different textile techniques like *kumihimo*, or braiding, about *shashiko* or padding, and about *kasuri* or *ikat*, a process also used in Mexico to dye *rebozos*. I took advantage of our long conversations to ask them about clothes and typical accessories that I saw used in daily life. I soon learned that paper fans weren't only used in summer but that they're a symbol of friendship and respect. So, when you present one to a friend before she goes on a trip, it's a sign of affection and, above all, respect. I asked them the names of things I didn't know, like *tabi*, the white socks shaped like rabbits' feet that women put on when they're wearing kimonos, or the *ashida*, the high-heeled wooden sandals that are worn when it rains. I learned to name things like *hanten*, a robe styled like a hip-length kimono used by men and women at parties, festivals, and even by salesmen to create more publicity for their companies' products. Because of this, on the back of the robe, you can see the logo of some business. And, something that

I didn't like until I learned its meaning was the *hachi-maki*, or better, a handkerchief that's tied around the head. They told me that when someone put it on, he or she promised from the bottom of his or her heart that any task undertaken, whether work, study, or whatever, would be done with all one's might. In effect, *isshokenmei*, or with all the blood that ran in your veins. All of this sounded so exciting that the days flew by.

Since it wasn't mandatory to go to school every day, Izumi, a very nice girl, attended classes twice a week. The other days she worked in an office, with computers, she said. She was intelligent, besides being an exceptional person. She sewed the finest suits; she took classes in everything and dressed in the latest fashions. Soon she became my friend. She was one of few I had there. One day she invited me to her home. It wasn't a simple invitation, no. We saw each other in the morning and she told me that she had a surprise for me, a visit to the Higashiyama zoo. She made sure that I hadn't been there so it would be a real adventure. The zoo was big and had very pretty gardens but it didn't seem out of this world to me although I never told her that. I was used to taking walks through Chapultepec Park from one end to the other and I don't know if it was just nostalgia but Mexico City always seemed grand to me. I missed those fountains in Chapultepec whose waters seemed like torrents and whose designs of serpents and Aztec gods demonstrated centuries of architectural expertise. As we walked, I kept noticing her impeccable manners. That day, out of pure carelessness, she'd forgotten her handkerchief. The Japanese never go out without a handkerchief; it's something essential, something as important as wearing the right dress. I took out some disposable ones and offered them to her. *Okotoba ni amaete,* she said to me softly. I didn't understand her words but understood what she was telling me. I memorized the phrase and used it in similar situations without knowing exactly what my lips were saying. Later I learned at school what it meant, *I grant myself the luxury of accepting your words* or, better, *your generosity.* Why does that expression sound so pedantic in Spanish or English when in Japanese it's like a delicate melody?

Izumi came from a place near Ichinomiya, which was famous for its production of wool and textiles. People from there would boast that they lived well; it wasn't necessary for them to add that it was because of the profits from those fabrics. Izumi explained to me about the importance of textiles in that area and also told me about Eisaku Noro when he still wasn't that well-known. According to her, Noro traveled from Japan to Australia and from there to Peru, Patagonia, and England in search of material. His first step was to choose a good product, whether angora, alpaca, or wool. He always did that with his eyes closed, feeling the material with just his fingertips. Later he took it to Japan to process it without any machines, only by hand, in order to produce a single thread or strand of yarn that was either soft, brilliant or lightweight. After that it was dyed using that legendary experience that the Japanese have of converting the dullest color into something divine. And, finally it was spun. That afternoon I realized that the Japanese knew about many things but out of respect never spoke too much about them because it was considered bad manners. Because of that, at the academy they'd explained little by little about how silk is made, from the moment the silk worm feeds on the mulberry leaves until it's boiled and cleaned with oxygenated water in order to remove the filaments and make a single thread.

Izumi's father was a businessman with a lot of money although he wasn't only interested in textiles. At night, he took us to an exclusive place that specialized in sushi. On the way home, her mother was waiting for us with French pastries and tea. Afterwards she told us that the bedrooms were ready. We went upstairs to the second floor and in the room, not only was there a perfectly-made bed but she'd prepared towels, pyjamas, and a toothbrush for me. I fell asleep and dreamed that my family and I were in the Tiradores Hacienda with my uncle Pascual. We'd eaten *carnitas* from Zinapécuaro, sea bass and young corn. We were in a rush. My father hurried us so we'd arrive quickly in Janitzio so he could buy a shawl for my mother. As we arrived in Janitzio, we were going uphill and eating more fish. I was awakened by Izumi's little alarm-clock in the adjoining room. It was eight in the morning and we had to have breakfast. Her mother offered us boiled eggs, sliced oranges, and toast. Izumi and her family begged me to return in July to experience the Festival of Tanabata, which takes place around the majestic Masumida temple. It's lovely to see the turtles in summer; besides, they sell crafts in the street and everything becomes so festive, her mother said. Before we left, they asked me if I wanted to go to her father's factory to see how robots worked. I told them I'd leave that for the next time. I left them, anxious to show my gratitude but I never returned.

The Fuji Academy organized a yearly fashion show where the students presented their best garments. The day of the show I presented a pair of skirts and a dress. During the event I noticed that I was the only young student who'd made clothing using the color purple. I'd drawn attention to the fabric's design because I mixed violet and white in a batik pattern. But unfortunately, in Japan that was a color for little old ladies. How strange: in that country, there were rules even for colors. A mature person couldn't dress in vibrant colors like red or yellow. So my tastes turned me into a *hen na gaijin*, a strange foreigner who ironically was a fervent admirer of Japanese culture. Why does everything turn out backwards for me? Nobody had warned me about it. I suppose that they wanted me to feel free and come up with designs that reflected my imagination. In the show it was clear that everyone had made exceptional pieces. Mine were more or less so. Well, less than more. The day of the show, more than fashion and the pieces' extravagance, I learned about organizing events. Everything had been prepared in an orderly and meticulous way, from the presentation of the garments to the meal that we ate right there after the program. Even during the rehearsal, hours before the show, everyone carried the laminated program in their hands to be sure that it didn't get wrinkled or tear. How did it occur to them to think about those things in advance? These lessons have been helpful to me till the present day. If my teacher and classmates only knew how grateful I still am. After the show the classes resumed. I left for Mexico. From there I wrote them. They all took up a collection and sent me a porcelain doll in an orange kimono. I lost it during one of my countless moves. All that remains for me is my memory of them and those stories that could never be repeated in a thousand years.

Araceli (front row, far right) with her classmates at the Fuji Academy; Professor Riu Tamiko (front row center), 1982.

Shisutā Shitī Feā
(Sister Cities Fair)

I didn't know what awaited me when I visited the Central Park, or
El Parque Central, for the first time. It wasn't very big, maybe twice
the size of the Alameda Central. Its design was rectangular and in
the middle there was an avenue that crossed it lengthwise, that is,
from north to south. In the distance you could see the *Terevitoo*, or the
Television Tower, in the heart of the park. It was an enormous tower
with an observatory and a restaurant which overlooked the city. I
kept walking along the main avenue, which was nothing special—to
the right, benches and to the left, the same thing. From the park,
you could enter the subway or, more accurately, the underground
city, where there were hundreds of stores and restaurants. That day,
I went down the stairs to get something to eat. I had a sandwich
and a cup of coffee. I exited the park from the opposite side and
as I reached the surface, I couldn't believe what I saw. To my right
were the spears of two very tall maguey plants, each more than a
yard high. They were surrounded by what appeared to be diorite
stones, like those used to make *metates* and *molcajetes*, only smooth-
er. They looked as if they'd been transported from the pyramids at
Teotihuacán. I guess they were put there to look pretty because, as
everyone knows, it's not necessary to surround magueys with stones.

Suddenly, to my left, I saw a huge stone about four yards
high. It was nothing less than a replica of the Aztec calendar. Behind
the calendar were two more monuments. To the right rose a figure
of the Tula warrior, shaped like a column. It was very tall. Well, it
looked very tall, maybe because it was standing in the park. Beneath
it was a plaque in Japanese and another in Spanish, explaining that

this column was a replica of one of those supporting the temple roof on the upper level of the pyramid at Tula, capital of the Toltec empire. Looking at it, I asked myself what would Japanese people think when they saw that warrior who wore a feather headdress, on his chest a butterfly coat-of-arms, who carried armor in one hand and an ornament in the other and, in back, as the final touch, the face of the sun-god on his belt-buckle. Such solemnity was comparable to the costumes and accessories of the ancient samurais whose extravagance led them to worship even the smallest detail, down to the elegant fastening of their belt-cords in back. Facing the warrior was a monument to Coyolxauhqui. The plaque explained that it represented the moon-goddess, the original of which had just been discovered in the excavations of the Templo Mayor.

So, three cultures were represented there: Aztec, Toltec, and Mexica. Those monuments were only there for that reason. Mexico City had donated them to the city of Nagoya to celebrate a friendship pact between both cities. In truth, in such matters, Mexico certainly outdoes itself. Why else ship enormous heavy monuments to the other side of the Pacific? And why the effort of sending a replica of Coyolxauhqui in 1980; hadn't the Templo Mayor just been discovered? I didn't know the reason but I still felt moved seeing such monuments in a city that had had little, very little, to do with Mexico. At least that was my first impression.

At the end of September, I was contacted by the Dentsu company and formally invited to their office, which was very close to the Central Park. They told me that the Shisutā Shitī Feā (Sister Cities Fair or Feria de Ciudades Hermanas—1982) was coming soon and that the municipality of Nagoya wanted me to be a guide for the Fair. Aha! Now I understood the reason for the monuments from Mexico and the importance of the "sister-cities" agreement. Nagoya had four sister cities: Los Angeles, Peking, Sydney, and Mexico City. To celebrate that friendship, the city was organizing cultural activities so that Japanese people could learn more about foreign cultures, apart from promoting the industries of the invited cities. They didn't ask me to be a guide because of my svelte body, no. As you know, guides are distinguished by their beauty and their stature. In my case, I had all the opposite qualities but to my fortune, I was one of the few Mexican women residing in the city. In fact, I only met one *tapatía* woman [from Guadalajara, Mexico] who'd lived there for some years. She was well established and had a family. She used to tell me that if she'd been given time to think it over, she might not have gotten married to a Japanese man or gone to live in his country. As if at bottom she were warning me, "don't make the same mistake as I did. . . ." But since I wasn't inclined toward or interested in that, I just listened to her attentively and respectfully.

It was strange that Nagoya was a "sister" of such different cities. Thinking about the past made me shiver. During the Second World War, Japan had attacked Australia, China, and the United States. One of the most sinister massacres took place when the Japanese occupied Peking. They committed almost unimaginable atrocities: fires, rapes, plunder and mutilations not only against military personnel but also civilians including women and children. About a quarter-of-a-million people died. But later history taught us that the Chinese weren't such saints either because they killed thousands of people in Tiananmen Square, just like the Mexicans did in Tlaltelolco. In the case of Australia, the Japanese bombed Darwin and attacked Sydney and Newcastle by submarine. As far as the United States, it's well known that the Japanese attacked Pearl Harbor, and to end the war once and for all, the Americans dropped nuclear bombs on Hiroshima and Nagasaki. But less is known about the concentration camps in California and other American states where the U.S. government imprisoned thousands of Japanese and Americans of Japanese descent. Enough said. Nobody needs lessons about the gringos' behavior before, during, and after the war. With that plague-ridden past, I asked myself how such friendship could be possible between those countries. I supposed that things can be forgiven but not forgotten. Those who lived through Mexico in 1968 [the Tlatelolco massacre] know more about these things.

The publicity for the Fair had begun downtown a month earlier. The organizers put up enormous signs with red and orange backgrounds whose white letters and images depicting the cities' names leapt out so that Japanese people could identify them easily. The symbol for Los Angeles was a luxury convertible, the one for Peking the imperial lions, the one for Sydney the opera house, and guess what was used for Mexico City? Well, of course: a mariachi. I couldn't deny it when I was asked dozens of times:

"Where are you from?"

"Mexico."

"Ah—from the land of the Los Panchos Trio."

In effect, Los Panchos had made their debut in Japan years before and were very well-known. For that reason, the image of a mariachi was most appropriate although I couldn't explain the difference between a trio and a real mariachi or anything about that musical style. When the city began mounting publicity for the Fair, the organizers called all the guides so we'd be downtown to give away balloons, caps and t-shirts, as if it were a political campaign. The media couldn't miss anything. The Japanese were sophisticated on that front: Everything was covered in the press, on radio and, above all, on TV. People worked fast and were informed about everything on the spot.

The Fair lasted two weeks and was held in a space similar to the Sports Palace.[3] Inside there were exhibitions where they displayed photos, diagrams, maps, models, and cultural artifacts from each country. Outside immense tents were set up for concerts and presentations. Each of the young guides was given a beautiful cherry-colored uniform made of cashmere. It was made up of a simple close-fitting dress, knee-length with long-sleeves, and included a bowler hat with a velvet band. We were also given a pink-and-white badge that was labeled *Guide* as well as with the name of each of our countries. Our job was to attend to the public in the area where the cultural artifacts were exhibited.

The Fair generated millions of yen because Japanese people were very curious and wanted to learn. Or viewed from a petty perspective, we could say that they went because there were few other places to go. I prefer to think that they attended out of a desire to have fun and to learn. The exposition was open all day and waves of students arrived in buses. There were also groups of old people, women, young couples, and who knows what other types of people. The fact is that the celebration was a true fair, like those in Mexico, but without flying carousels, or a wheel of fortune, or stuffed eggs,[4] or confetti, or fried snacks, and of course there weren't any exploding little bulls.

Between photos, lectures, and good conversations, I learned a lot from that experience. Before that I'd known very little about Australia. In fact, the Fair took place barely ten years since the opening of the Sydney Opera House, that elegant building shaped like a sailing ship and finished with white glazed tiles. Years later, that structure became famous all over because of the Olympics but at that time, I didn't know anything about it. I learned that the opera house not only presented opera but also classical music, ballet, pop and rock in different theaters and auditoriums inside it. I also learned

---

3   The Sports Palace is a huge arena that is used for both national and international exhibits and sports competitions in Mexico City.

4   Eggs whose contents have been emptied and re-filled with flour; people smash these on each other's heads at fairs.

about the Tiwi, the aboriginal people who live on Bathurst and Melville islands. They celebrate a highly complex burial ceremony called *pukumani*. Much of their art relates to this ritual. They paint impressive totem-poles and place them around the tomb. For the Tiwi, those poles are like human figures related to the deceased. I also heard about the painters Tom Roberts and Russell Drysdale. Drysdale's paintings made me think of the Mexican muralists because of their themes and maybe their style, and in some way they were all influenced by abstract and surrealist painting. A reproduction of his painting "Shopping Day" moved me because it depicted aborigines, inhabitants of North Queensland, with empty hands. Even from a distance the figures' hunger, desolation, and suffering were obvious. Just as in Mexico you see so many indigenous people torn from their villages and struggling in the big cities for a scrap of bread, the aborigines in Drysdale's portrayals look isolated, as if facing exploitation and marginalization in their own land. Several of his paintings are like that, intense and heartrending.

There's no doubt that there's poverty everywhere and there are parts of our respective histories that we'd like to erase. Australia was discovered by the English at a time when it was home to thousands of aborigines who'd populated the place for centuries. With the arrival of the English colonizers, hunger, exploitation, and disease killed off half the natives in short order. This happened more than 200 years ago, almost at the same time that England lost its biggest colony: the United States. And, since the British didn't have any other place to send so many drunks, pickpockets, rapists, and murderers, they decided to populate Sydney with those convicts. So the first Australian city was mostly colonized by criminals and a handful of police officers to guard them. To top it off, the official navy was made up of what were called "the rum police," because they had a monopoly on that tasty Caribbean spirit. Their story is very common. They were exploiters who lived off cheap labor and with the profits they gleaned from alcohol, they built houses huge as palaces. But it wasn't all exploitation, drunkenness and prostitution; in time the convicts were freed and the country prospered in spite of that and its "White Australian Law," which stipulated that only white Europeans could live there. Years later I realized that, far from expressing shame over the past, the great works of Australian literature and history forgive the mistakes of their ancestors because they openly describe their roots and misconceptions.

When you're Mexican, you feel that you know North American cities as if you'd been born in them. I'm not sure if that's because

Mexicans have watched a lot of American TV or because they often have family members or other people they know up north. At the Fair there was information about "The People of Our Lady the Queen of the Porciuncula Angels" or, as it's better known, Los Angeles, and its founding by the Spanish in 1781. It wasn't mentioned that the city became part of Mexico in 1821 or that Mexico lost it in 1848 because of the U.S. intervention. But anyway, what attracted the most attention was the information about the film industry and aviation in the twenties: Hollywood and the founding of the studios in 1911; Hollywood Boulevard and the stars incrusted on the pavement with the names of famous actors who left their mark there; Graumann's Chinese Theater, famous for movie premieres; Universal Studios, Walt Disney, the San Fernando Valley, Sunset Boulevard, etcetera. It's a familiar story for us as close neighbors.

The Chinese exhibition presented a giant map of Peking, which delineated in great detail the walls of the Imperial City, with its monumental doors that protect the Forbidden City. Inside this there were palaces, temples, statues, marble staircases, and the imposing temple of Confucius. Seeing the map reminded me of the Zócalo in Mexico City, and I wondered what would have happened if the Aztecs had built a wall around Tenochtitlán. For some reason, the Forbidden City made me think of the first *plano*, or historical center, of Mexico City. With the discovery of the Coyolxauhqui, the Templo Mayor project had just started. Each discovery promised a splendor lived only by our ancestors. There were photos on display of the palaces and towers of the Forbidden City. These had golden roofs that contrasted with the stairs and balustrades built out of white marble. And, from north to south was a string of arched doorways and patios and more patios until you could see the immense throne-room. That architectural wonder took away your breath. Does the traveler to Mexico have the same sensation when he or she visits Teotihuacán, Tula or Chichén-Itzá? Although I learned about Peking only through photos and models, that was enough for me to appreciate some of its history.

When you're raised in a city without rivers, you grow up worshipping those that have them. The map illustrated that, apart from temples, Peking was filled with parks, forests, cemeteries, and above all, rivers and canals. For that reason, that city which was so unknown to me, made me think about ancient Mexico City, which I also hadn't known. I'd grown up reading and hearing that Mexico City was founded on an islet that was expanded by means of man-made islands which led to canals that connected houses, palaces, temples, markets and aqueducts. Just as Tenochtitlán was connected with the valley by means of causeways that ran north in the direction of Tepeyac, west en-route to Xochimilco, and eastward toward Tlacopan, the Chinese also built temples outside the Forbidden City that connected those cardinal points: to the north that of the earth, to the south the sky, to the west the moon, and to the east the sun.

But the photos that most attracted my attention were those of the Temple of Heaven and that of the Summer Palace built next to the Kunming Lake, where the emperors lived during the summer season. The scenes of the Ming tombs were my favorite because of their grandeur. They were a series of mausoleums, each one set within an amphitheater of mountains toward which ran a wide avenue flanked by immense marble statues shaped like animals. There were twelve kinds of animals represented in pairs. The lion statues were the most impressive for their aura of strength and dignity. That's where I learned about the importance of the lion as a guardian, above all in sacred places. For that reason, it wasn't excessive for Peking to have donated to Nagoya two marble pedestals with yards-high lions on them. These served as a portico since they were located at one of the entranceways to the Central Park, very close to the Aztec calendar and the Coyolxauhqui.

At the Fair, there were tents outside where shows were staged. The performances from China and Mexico attracted huge crowds. The Chinese brought a group of acrobats and jugglers of all ages. Although some were still children, it was obvious that they'd been professionally trained to leap, contort their bodies, balance objects and produce a first-class show. They formed human pyramids and balanced upside-down but their most amazing feat of agility was the dance of the dragons, whose fire-red, green and golden masks and bodies were displayed almost magically. From Mexico came a little-known group, one of those that used to tour through Japanese towns and cities, the Tres Amigos Trio. They were dressed in modern *charro* suits, garishly red with white patterns that looked as if they were made of silk, their flared pants subtly matching them. Their bow ties, which were also made of a white, sleek material, were finely embroidered with metallic thread. The button-holes on their suits were shaped like owls' faces; their belts embroidered leather with white studs. Their show was the liveliest one.

Since I always liked to present myself well, I asked my mother to send me a traditional Mexican dress, any one, any one at all, as long as it were traditional. I dreamed about appearing in a *jicapextle*-style *tehuana* costume with a *huipil* blouse, the skirt abundantly embroidered with flowers. I'd never worn one but Leti, my older sister, had. I'd always been fascinated by the whiteness of the *esplendor* head-cloth and the contrast of those fine velvets embroidered with motifs of Oaxacan nature. But to my surprise, my mother sent me a *china poblana* costume, which ended up showing off better, not because it was prettier than the *tehuana* costume but because people love to see dresses completely embroidered with sequins and beads. She didn't send me a *rebozo* but I had one and put it on. It didn't match but who cared? I felt like the queen of the Fair when in the afternoon I went up to the stage to dance a *zapateada* while the Trio sang a typical *ranchera*. What emotion! From the time I was a young girl in school, I'd always recited and, thanks to the exceptional programs that teach Mexican children folk dancing and how to dress in traditional costumes, that stage in Japan was only an extension of who I was. How grateful I felt at that moment to my parents and teachers.

As part of the preparation and the programming at the Fair, the organizers called on Japanese specialists of different cultures to contribute their knowledge. That's how I met Master Itō Takayoshi, a true *aficionado* of Mexican culture. In fact, a good number of the artifacts presented in the Mexico exposition belonged to him. One day he arrived very early carrying two large suitcases. "I see that you like dresses. Why don't you put on a different one today?" he asked me. Then he began to take out *huipiles* from Oaxaca of all different shades, including ones with ribbons; a dress from Chiapas with a double-skirt embroidered with silk thread; from Guerrero he brought Amuzgo *huipiles* and *chilena* skirts with gorgeous beadwork; from Hidalgo a *quezquemetetl* cape, and a skirt embroidered with cross-stitching; and I couldn't miss the one from Veracruz, elegant with its skirt of organza, its velvet apron, and lace mantilla. He also had dresses from the north: one from Jalisco with its double-skirt, ribbons and lace; one from Durango with lovely embossed fabric; and two from Tamaulipas, one with a wide, "polka"-style skirt, and another close-fitting, in suede, with white patterns. For the first time I realized that dresses from central and southern Mexico are loose-fitting while those from northern Mexico are snug, at least from the waist up. Besides that, one is flashy, extravagant, with flora and fauna that seem to overflow from the borders of the cloth; the other is generally made with simple colors or with material that's lightly embossed. There's no doubt that a dress reflects the history, ambience, creativity, and the shape of the body. We women from central and southern Mexico are on the short side and roundish, while those from northern Mexico are tall and svelte.

I couldn't stand the temptation and I asked Master Itō to lend me the dress from Yucatán. It was a *huipil* and skirt made of a fabric that felt like silk but was a blend of polyester and cotton and hand-embroidered with purple, red, and yellow flowers, ending in tulle. These were definitely not dresses from La Lagunilla or from markets like those in San Cosme or Tacuba. They were dresses he'd bought in each region. Whenever possible, he bought them directly from the *campesinos* themselves, he told me. Since the Master was a painter, on his trips to Mexico, he brought his daughter, Saori, so she could learn from indigenous people how to weave and embroider on a loom. Saori gave a presentation at the Fair to teach Japanese people how cloth is spun in Mexico. Both spoke in a broken Spanish, like many indigenous Mexicans. It was interesting and also understandable that they spoke with a Oaxacan accent, which I believe they'd acquired over there, maybe by Juchitán.

I asked Master Itō how many dresses he owned. Too many to count, he told me. Stuttering in amazement, I also asked him why dresses attracted him so much and he answered that since he was a painter, beauty pleased him; afterwards he started to collect them and, with time, fell in love with them. I wanted to ask him what he planned to do with so many of them but he wisely read my thoughts and spoke before I could, saying that he'd been thinking of building a museum of popular Mexican culture in Nagoya. What gracious, sincere work, I thought. I felt proud. There's no doubt that the Fair was a great history lesson. And so I continued learning, pleased to see and hear the appreciation the people there had for me, that they had for us Mexicans in that far-flung place. I felt that my life was like a dress that's being spun little by little, and that for me every stitch was not only a lesson but a fresh surprise.

Promoting the Sister Cities Fair, 1982.

Wearing the China Poblana dress at the Fair, 1982.

Wearing a Yucateca dress borrowed from artist Itō Takayoshi's collection, 1982.

Ninjin to Tamago
(A Carrot and an Egg)

Little cooking was done in the house where I lived. Toshi-chan made his own breakfast at 8:15 in the morning. He ate rice, dried seaweed, and spoiled beans. Okay, okay, let's take things a little slower, what's this about spoiled beans? Well, as a matter of fact, there's a very strange dish that's called *nattō* and it's made of fermented soybeans. I made an attempt to eat those sticky, slimy, and smelly beans that surely are eaten with mustard and scallions but I never could until one day my friends invited me to a house in the country, in Shizuoka, near Mount Fuji.

That day we arrived at 4 in the afternoon and from that time until we left to bathe (one by one, of course, please don't get ahead of me), in a wooden tub out in the elements, the lady of the house served us at least twenty small dishes. We ate all night. She didn't stop cooking and never sat down at the table with us. In that house, they did everything the old-fashioned way. The lady of the house was there to serve and never leave the kitchen. The next day, in the morning, she'd already gotten up very early and was waiting for us with the table set for our breakfast. She offered us soup, a piece of grilled salmon, rice, seaweed, and *nattō*. As much as I'd refused to eat those awful beans, I'd have to eat the ones there. I felt obliged to the lady. I felt I don't know what; like when you don't know how to thank such effort, such generosity. I don't know if it was something magical, a way to say thank-you, a gift from God, or what they call style or gratitude, but I ate those beans as if they were nothing, and even finished with the appropriate expression: *oishikatta desu*, everything was delicious. Or was it that I was already becoming Japanese and you always had to say *oishikatta desu*? I don't know. I never loved *nattō* but I began to eat it without repulsion. People said that eating *nattō* was the most difficult test for foreigners to pass.

In the mornings, I had breakfast with Toshi-chan only a few times. I would eat a Western-style breakfast a little later with Kimiko. I put it like that to use a name that sounds pleasant or rather sophisticated. Yes, it's worth a good laugh. I won't be offended if you laugh at my pseudo-vocabulary. It was a simple meal: coffee with milk and two slices of buttered toast. Most of the time bread came in gigantic slices, twice the thickness as what was served in Mexico. It was delightful. Since we'd always been bread-eaters in my home, breakfast was just about my favorite meal of the day. We were three strange beings. Each one ate on his or her own. Each made his or her own things. We were a family because we lived together but the truth is that we had practically nothing in common. Toshi-chan ate in his company's dining room. Kimiko in some restaurant, and I, in order not to spend money, half the time in a restaurant and the other half alone at home. I used to prepare some Maruchan-style *rāmen* or a meal to take with me that I ate at school. It wasn't a big deal: rice with some ham or some kind of sausage and some vegetable on hand. That portable meal is called *bentō*. And, like many things in Japan, the *bentō* has to be prepared like a work of art or an artist's painting. Everything must be arranged to match perfectly as far as color, the shape of the *bentō* box, the way you eat the things inside it. I learned that you never should place a green vegetable next to another the same color because the colors will get lost. On the other hand, a green vegetable next to a carrot is fine because the green stands out against the orange. You also must keep matching everything that surrounds the rice. That is, you have to create a kind of garden whose colors harmonize the beauty of each flower while at the same time the whole group resembles a perfect work of art. *Bentō* boxes are more or less 6 by 8 inches. At times I would put in rice and on the side some small fish, like *charales;* then, a boiled egg and two or three pickled vegetables. Sometimes it wasn't that elaborate; I put in rice and some kind of meat, usually leftovers from the day before. But it wasn't as easy as putting *chile* on a tortilla. No. It was making sure that everything looked just right, perfect. A pleasing combination of colors and shapes was imperative.

But in Mexico we don't grow up ignoring those things because our cuisine is also very artistic. That's why we put lettuce, cheese, cream, and sliced radishes on top of golden-brown *taquitos,* on top of *huaraches, quesadillas* and all other kinds of snacks. We mix green, white, and red not because we're such patriots and think about the verdant laurel of victory or about white lilies or about the blood our heroes spilled. No. We mix them simply because in addition to being nutritious, they're exquisite and go perfectly well with soft or fried tortillas, and not only that but our cuisine is also a garden but a very Mexican garden where perfection gets in the way but where the colors almost lend it a lovely shape, a baroque shape, as wise men would say.

So I carried my meals with me every once in a while, which was very Japanese but with a Mexican touch. We hardly ate at home so we hardly bought anything. I would open the refrigerator and there was milk, butter, *chamoy*, some kind of fish, pickled vegetables and tangerines, by some chance. . . . Sometimes our schedules coincided and we were all home at meal-time. Then Kimiko said, let's eat at home. And I thought to myself, "and what does she think we're going to eat if there's only *ninjin to tamago* in the refrigerator?" In effect, there were only carrots and an egg. She put on rice to cook. She fried the egg and cut it into pieces. Then, she cut up the carrot, also into pieces, and fried it, too. When it was almost done, she added the rice and the egg. It turned into a delicious fried rice. . . . and all she added was salt! And if that weren't enough, she prepared a soup only with tiny dried fish eggs that she kept in a little jar. It was just a clear broth but tasted marvelous. That was our meal. Dinner was another matter, above all because it was the main meal of the day and we ate it outside, at work, already late, after nine at night. When clearly there wasn't even a carrot around, she put on rice to cook and when it was ready, we beat an egg and tossed on soy sauce. Then we took some dried seaweed, like *hojaldre* leaves but dark green, and stuffed them with rice as if they were *taquitos*, and just like that we dipped them into a raw-egg and soy-sauce mixture. That was our meal. What?! Seaweed with rice and a raw egg? Maybe it sounds disgusting to you but not to me. Don't tell me that the Japanese aren't disgusted by the thought of certain people in Mexico stopping at street stands and tossing down a sherry with a raw egg on an empty stomach. To each his own. To each her own.

I never told anyone about those frugal meals we made from time to time at home. No one would have believed it. I can just imagine: "What? That's all they eat? So rich and so cheap. . . ! So what do they do with so much money? What miserable people!" I anticipated all the things they'd say. Of course, it was a wealthy home but an impoverished life, or let's say, an economical one lived there. That was done on purpose—well, the matter of not taking care of ourselves and nobody buying food was our own fault—but living a simple life every day was a philosophy for them. And I don't want to brag about it by using highbrow words; the matter is simpler than it seems. I remember one time my uncle in Michoacán told me that the *campesinos* who helped him would carry salt, tortillas, and some kind of *chile* to the fields during the sowing season. Since they spent hours and hours in the fields, they had to eat cold tortillas, just like that with salt and *chiles*. That was their meal. They had no other choice. They weren't given time to return home and at least eat warm tortillas. And those people were so humble that at times they ate only scraps of pork spread over tortillas and they spent days and weeks that way. In the countryside that's how life goes and it's known all too well that there are people, although not just in the country, who live on tortillas spread with beans or potatoes. So for the Japanese, at least for the couple I lived with, it was necessary to eat simple food every day to be able to have a good time when you went out to eat. Then yes, nothing about measuring, nothing about worrying about prices and even less about the *sake* or the beers, or the wine that you drank. You sat down leisurely to eat everything. "Because of that, one must live poor every day in order to truly enjoy when you go out to eat," they told me. "If you sat down to eat like a king every day, you couldn't appreciate life when you leave your house," they told me repeatedly.

Although Tochi-chan and Kimiko had grown up in families with money, they'd been victims of the Second World War. Both remembered the sound of the bombs, the massacres, the ambulances, the shrieks, the moans. They remembered how they were put under the table with pillows over their heads so the bombs wouldn't burst their eardrums. They spoke little about that but I knew it had caused them a lot of pain. They grew up in the middle of a Japan that had suffered the errors and horrors of combat. Exactly. They were condemned to grow up eating the equivalent of cold tortillas with salt and, when things were going well for them, they could also eat scraps. This was their daily meal: rice with a salted chunk of whale blubber. They filled themselves up, they grew up hating whale and that horrifying meal served at school every day. But what could they do? The country was in ruins and they had to eat out of hunger and nothing more. And as much as they hated their situation and their suffering, that was their best school, the best school of their lives. Forget about home economics or any other kind of class. There they'd learned to save and to not waste anything, anything, not even things left to spoil. Because of this, for them, frugal meals were, if not nostalgia for difficult times, then the memory that you should and can live life modestly to be sure that you'll always have savings. I learned that from them. I learned it by heart. I began to invent little dishes made with only a single medium-sized squash. I learned to not waste anything.

Akirame ga warui! In June 1945, many Japanese were convinced that they were going to lose the war. Among them, there were two factions. One group began a campaign to convince the leaders to surrender once and for all before the United States and its allies defeated them. The other faction was made up of militants and nationalists who'd also realized that they were going to lose but didn't know how to convince themselves of that reality. They were completely traumatized. In the upper echelons of the army, meetings and more meetings took place and strategies were discussed to bring an end to the war until one day an officer shouted, *Akirame ga warui! We don't know how to surrender!* For the military, fighting in the war was an order they'd received. So, allowing themselves to be defeated was equivalent to betraying their government and their people. Japan was at the point of losing a war for the first time in its history but since they didn't know how to surrender because of questions of honor, respect, a feudal psychology that was part of them, they continued fighting until the atomic bombs put an end to all that in August 1945.

Just as with the war, the Japanese don't know how to surrender once they've undertaken a project. That sentiment of *Akirame ga warui! We don't know how to surrender!* became palpable after the war, when the country lay in ashes and it was necessary to begin rebuilding it. That generation of children and young people, victims of the war, had to work day and night and didn't surrender until they saw their country developed again, secure and in peace. The war left that generation with an open wound that never healed. No, Kimiko and Toshi-chan didn't complain about what they'd suffered but the way they lived and saved money showed that they weren't willing to squander what so much work had cost them to achieve. Kimiko was from Kyoto, from a good family that lived on the shores of the Kamo River, very close to Gion, the *geisha* district. In other words, she was from a family that was very well-to-do until the war came. When the country was rebuilding itself, they had to move to Nagoya because there were more opportunities there. That's where she started her first business and worked non-stop for more than twenty years. It was curious because among themselves the Japanese make fun of the natives of Nagoya. They accuse them of being skin-flints, boring, people without culture. Kimiko, at bottom from Kyoto, also complained about them although it was there where she recovered her fortune. She spoke with a typical Kyoto accent to be sure that others realized whom they were contending with, a person from Kyoto itself, the ancient capital of Japan. To top it off, when giving thanks, she said *ōkini* instead of the usual *arigatō*. But, as far as saving money, she was like people from Nagoya because she only knew how to work, work, work and save, save, save.

One had to calculate everything; what you were going to spend in a day, in a week, in a month, in a year. If you had a budget of 1,000 yen a day, you adjusted to that and not a penny more. Life in Japan was very expensive and you had to stick to your budget. That is, there weren't laws stipulating that but if anyone exceeded his or her limit, it looked very bad. Food was ridiculously expensive, especially meat and fruit. So that you had to keep alternating between noodles one day, rice another, fish the next, then tofu and that's how it went. What you had to protect with all your strength was the amount of money you were willing to save every month. That was not to be touched for anything in the world. It was sacred.

When I arrived in Japan, one day my friends saw me pulling out the inside of a roll. They were very surprised. "Why are you taking out the center?" they asked. Because it's fattening, I answered unequivocally. "Well if it's fattening, eat half the bread but don't waste it. *Mottainai*! What a waste!" On one level I felt offended but I soon realized that for them waste was their worst enemy. Because of that they ate even if it were only a carrot and an egg. Everything had to be measured, guarded, and enjoyed at the same time. No eating until you were full, no throwing away leftovers, no letting things spoil. They repeated to exhaustion that I had to stop eating when I still felt a little hungry. Imagine that. For me that was like telling me, "stop eating before the beans and dessert are brought out." So, no. I didn't come from the same stock. I was used to eating until I was full, well, at least that's how they taught me at home. Besides, since my parents had their own business, we sat down to eat between 3:00 and 5:30 in the afternoon. We always ended with a nice dessert and some *café con leche*, which my mother always liked. But for the Japanese, eating too much was not so much a bad habit but a sign that you were harming your body. That's the reason they were so frugal when they ate, to keep themselves slender and healthy. Well, they explained it in every way possible but I still didn't understand and even less so my stomach.

In Japan women control one-hundred percent of the house expenses. That's an agreement that's kept, understood, and respected.

In the house where I lived the marriage was, let's say, one of convenience. They'd married without love, only so they wouldn't be alone. He earned a lot of money but she earned more. It wasn't a typical family in any sense because he managed his own expenses, and she, hers. I contributed with a rather symbolic amount. We were like three friends living under the same roof. That's when I realized that Japanese men are also very cautious and thrifty. Instead of going out to drink with his buddies when it wasn't absolutely necessary, Toshi-chan would return home early, drink a beer and eat some snack. Then he sat out on the balcony to watch the city. He didn't spend money on anything foolish. He didn't smoke and to his good fortune, he didn't even spend anything at the golf-matches he liked so much. Since his work was so important, to entertain his clients, he took them to play golf and the expenses were covered by his company. He always lost on purpose to make his clients happy, so they'd feel important. That's how he did his business, disguised as a loser. And he returned home with bottles and more bottles of whiskey that they gave him as gifts. He put them in a closet and that was that. He wasn't interested in drinking them. He didn't have a car because he thought that walking to work or taking the subway once in a while was more wholesome. He lived a completely healthy and thrifty life.

Kimiko, his wife, was like him but in her own way. At her company, the workers spoke very badly about her, because according to them, she was very cheap. And the truth is that she was because she never let go of even one cent. She never did anything for anyone, either. She never offered anyone a discount, not even her best client. I just looked and listened but kept my mouth shut. But without realizing it, I started becoming more and more like him, like her, in the way I spent money, or to put it better, didn't spend it; I saved instead. It was one of two things: either they had money because they were cheap or because they were careful and made sure they saved. I'd like to think that they held onto their money because of their great suffering during their childhood and adolescence. It was very obvious that Japanese people squandered money when they went out to dinner or on the town but during the course of a normal day they were very careful with their expenses. I didn't live in a normal house because we lived much better than most people. Kimiko had exquisite taste and since the penthouse was half Western and half Eastern because the floors of the bedrooms were covered with *tatami* mats, she made sure to furnish it with pieces bought in Europe and Asia. Her dishes were Japanese and Spanish, while the cutlery was made of pure silver from India. She'd traveled to Islamabad to buy her rugs and to Istanbul to have her lamps made. She had Chinese furniture, Moroccan mirrors, Australian animal-skins and a world of objects. "When you go to Mexico you'll go crazy from our handicrafts," I kept telling her. On the other hand, I had the chance to visit many regular houses and apartments. There I realized that people lived in much smaller spaces and since energy was so expensive, they were rigorously careful with gas and electricity. Air conditioning was a true luxury. And, although people had money to spend, they preferred to live without things rather than touch their savings.

I left Japan with the hope of returning and establishing myself there one day. I returned casually years later, not to remain there but on a visit. Japan was already drastically changing. The young people now didn't have the same values as the generation of Kimiko and Toshi-chan, those victims of the war. Now the youth were using credit cards and surrendering to the mania of spending carelessly. They were buying suits and bags and motorbikes and cars even knowing that they didn't have funds to cover them. They began to go into debt in a way never seen before. The culture of saving and of intense work without rest began to disappear. But that transformation was above all most severe for the parents and grandparents of those young people. With their lifetime savings they had to pay the consequences. Those funds they'd amassed with such effort had to be used to pay for the whims of a youth that didn't understand what this finally meant: *Akirame ga warui!* Just the opposite. Those young people did know how to surrender. They either couldn't or didn't know how to pay the debts from their fancies. I suppose that this happens everywhere, not just in Japan. What I learned from Kimiko and Toshi-chan has no price.

With Tezuka Kimiko,
1984.

Tezuka Toshimasa,
1984.

A room in the Tezuka penthouse,
1984.

Sabetsu
(Discrimination)

Sometimes I felt like a dog on the way to the crematorium. I would wake up feeling so sad. I felt abandoned. I was falling into what they now call "the *depre*," although at that time we didn't use that word. I felt homesick, incredibly so and it made me want to return to Mexico. It wasn't easy to call long distance by telephone; or rather, it was easy but super-expensive. I used to go to the central office and every minute cost a fortune. When I couldn't stand it any longer, I went to the Central Park to take a walk. I would see the same people moving in the same direction. Everything looked gray and dull. I remember that a man walked his white dog every day. It was gigantic, a Borzoi, a Russian dog that attracted a lot of attention because of its size and elegance. When I felt bad, I distracted myself with them and for a few moments forgot my sadness.

One day I realized that in Japan there weren't really any street dogs. It seemed strange to me because, as it's known, in Mexico, they're everywhere. In fact I ended up owning a dog that had wandered all over the city until it depended on us because I'd begun feeding it. I gave him only scraps, different kinds of soup that I invented with tortillas and bones but in the end, had a little bit of everything in it . . . He wasn't at all pretty. He was one of those mutts, medium-sized with little fur, half-brown, half-grayish. God only knows how old he was; at that time I never wondered about such things. I soon felt affection for him and loved him from the bottom of my heart. He followed me everywhere. But in Japan street dogs weren't tolerated. Once I heard that they were often poisoned and their bodies made to disappear. I never took it seriously, although it was obvious that there simply weren't any dogs without owners on the street. In some way, people must have wanted the city to look clean, almost antiseptic.

There also weren't any beggars or poor people. I never saw them. I suppose that since the economy was so strong at the beginning of the eighties, there simply weren't any people that poor. It's surprising because just thirty-five years earlier, the Japanese had lived in the worst poverty that one could imagine. Many lost their homes and family members during the war. It was as if they had to step over their own ashes. They had to stand hunger, cold, torrential rain and heat. They were ruined and the city was an encampment of the sick, nomads, orphans, insane and sad people. But revenge, complete revenge, finally came. Through work and years of deprivation, by saving money and effort, they emerged from that rubble. Now they enjoyed a lifestyle that was too good to be true.

Kibishii. Japanese society is *kibishii.* It's strict. It always has been. People who stray from the norm pay a very high price. Just like little soldiers, children and adolescents must go to school; at least until high school. And in order to enter the university, they're given some very difficult exams that it takes them years to study for. Their parents even spend a fortune on special schools called *juku,* which prepares them so they don't fall behind and they can compete to take those exams. Sometimes they spend years taking classes that are intentionally given in the afternoon or at night, after school and even on weekends. Once students pass those exams, their future is clear. A good grade on an exam can guarantee admission to a prestigious university which means that the young man or woman will get a good job, a good position, and as a result an excellent salary. But there are kids who can't bear the pressure and before they can take the exams, commit suicide. Others can't handle the strictness of the system and leave school. These are called *ochikobore* or "those left behind." No one is forgiven. There isn't even compassion for those who aren't capable of learning quickly. Once a young person quits school, he or she can't get back into the system. And, even if they enroll in night school or an open high school, these young people will never have the same opportunities again. They remain marked for life and are condemned to accept the lowest kind of jobs. As if that weren't enough, the jobs that they're given lack decent benefits or aren't even permanent. They pass through life from contract to contract, with little security and, of course, earning low salaries. Although they say that both education and work benefits are changing for these people, in any case, things continue being *kibishii.*

To this class of people belong the day-laborers—in other words, bricklayers—who generally work in construction. When I lived in Nagoya, they lived in neighborhoods crowded with single men. Every day, those workers were given an assigned job in a specific location called *yoseba*, where they were picked up if there was work for them. As happens with so many bricklayers in Mexico, their work was very dangerous and they didn't have health insurance. And of course in Japan there were also accidents that happened more often than not. Only that you never learned more about this sort of thing; it was never reported. I even heard that the Olympic Stadium in Tokyo was built thanks to the manual labor of thousands and thousands of day laborers. Those neighborhoods were concentrated in the southern part of Nagoya. The bricklayers always had a bad reputation, above all because loneliness and poverty drove them to ruin. They drank too much, gambled what they didn't have, and frequented the lowest brothels and the worst bars.

Japan was always severe. In fact, there existed and still exists a system called *koseki*, a kind of family registry which everyone must sign up for by law. Everything is recorded in that file, the name, place and date of birth, date of marriage, divorce, adoption, legitimate and illegitimate children. Every little thing. And, on top of that, the registry is public. Or maybe, until the middle of the '70s, anyone had access to that data, but now it's not so easy to see it if you don't have a good reason. In reality, that was and still can be a double-edged sword. It's good for those who are getting married and want to be sure that their partners are available, free of problems or commitments. Company managers and school personnel also end up having recourse to those administrative registries in order to ensure that a candidate or student to be admitted has a stainless record. Unfortunately, that registry is an obstacle for those in marginalized groups because the more the common citizenry is informed about those individuals' ancestors, the more they can be denied work. In other words, it discriminates indirectly.

There have always been marginalized people in Japan. I remember that one Sunday we went into the subway and before us were seated four Korean girls. They were beautifully dressed in traditional costumes from their country, or *hanbok*, as they're called. They were wearing loose-fitting skirts down to their ankles and above, long-sleeved blouses with "V" necks. The colors of their silk dresses were gorgeous: lime-green, lilac, pink—almost Mexican pink—and one of them yellow. Surely these young girls, who weren't more than eighteen, were going to or returning from some ceremony that merited such costumes. I was fascinated and got lost admiring all the details of their gorgeous outfits. Suddenly I felt the powerful gaze of Kimiko, who was disdainfully looking only at their feet. "Look at them, how ridiculous!," she deliberately said out loud, so they'd hear her. I didn't understand at the time why she felt such contempt for those young girls she didn't even know, for those young women who were so beautiful and so well-dressed, worthy of a photograph in an album. Eventually I understood that the Japanese and the Koreans had always fought like cats and dogs.

Japan and Korea are neighboring countries, just as Mexico is a neighbor (by misfortune or not) of the United States. It turns out that a hundred years ago, Japan owned Korea and allowed Koreans who left their country to work and live in Japan. The Koreans were almost always temporary laborers because, although they were allowed to work unconditionally, they were given the most physically demanding jobs. From the beginning they were looked down on, even when there was a mega-earthquake in Tokyo, around in 1923, and under the pretext of a rumor accusing Koreans of having poisoned the wells, thousands and thousands of them were murdered. As if that weren't enough, when the Second World War came, the Japanese forced the Koreans to work in factories and mines. During the war, the Japanese always were severe. They wanted to win the war at all costs, so they put a high price on, among other things, the manual labor carried out by the Koreans, who were at the mercy of what they could offer the Japanese army. When Japan lost the war, it had to get rid of Korea. Thousands of Koreans returned to their country where, by the way, the situation was also a disaster. Put differently, they went from the frying pan into the fire. And in spite of the fact that the Japanese situation was devastating, at least a half-million Koreans decided to remain in Japan. Then Korea was divided in two and, well, that history is too long to recount here. The fact is that the Koreans who live in Japan today were born in Japan and speak Japanese as their first language. But the Japanese government doesn't recognize them as Japanese citizens but only as foreign residents even if they were born on Japanese soil.

It was a story of love and hate. The Japanese constantly bad-mouthed Koreans. Ah! But not Korean cuisine because they loved to eat in their restaurants. There was a very busy neighborhood near the Imaike metro station that had clothing and shoe stores with enormous discounts. There were lots of *nomiya* or cantinas with delicious snacks; there were little corners where they grilled wheat-balls with octopus, called *takoyaki*. As far as you looked, there were red streetlamps announcing traditional food and drink. Along the sidewalks of the major avenues that faced north, south, east and west, there were hundreds of bicycles; the eye couldn't take them all in. Many people were accustomed to going shopping by bicycle. It was one of the oldest and liveliest neighborhoods in Nagoya. Everyone was used to going shopping there until the luxury shops were built around the Central Park, in the city center.

It was delightful to visit the Imaike district because it gave you the sensation of living in the past. My friends and I would go there because it had the best Korean restaurants. One Korean specialty was what the Japanese call *yakiniku* or grilled beef. We gorged ourselves on that tender meat that melted in your mouth. The curious thing was that the Koreans ate *chile* like in Mexico and seasoned their dishes with many of the spices we also used. Once the meat was grilled it was dipped in a sauce made from dried *chile* with garlic, soy sauce, oil and scallions. Sometimes the meat was marinated the night before in a similar kind of sauce; then sesame seeds and oil were mixed in. But the meat wasn't eaten by itself, it was accompanied by rice, pickled vegetables, lettuce and *charales* or some other kind of very spicy fish. Why did the Koreans eat so differently from the Japanese? Why did they seem so much like us? They would also put meat, spicy vegetables and even cilantro onto a lettuce-leaf and then roll it as if it were a taco. I told myself, the only difference is that they use lettuce instead of tortillas; maybe that's why they were so thin.

Ninniku kusai! They stink of garlic! the Japanese used to say. And the truth is that the Koreans were obsessed with garlic; they even used to eat it raw. I'd heard that bullfighters also ate raw garlic to stay slim. But the Koreans used to say it was good for the circulation and the skin. So just imagine how that traumatized women who ate raw garlic on an empty stomach. Besides that, they had some recipes which sounded half-macabre with black garlic and home remedies like those sold in the Sonora Market. On the other hand, they had exquisite soups that, except for the lack of *epazote* and corn, I could swear tasted like a delicious *mole de olla*. They even made one with beef-bones, cabbage, soybeans and cow's blood to cure hangovers. I imagined *sopa de médula, pancita,* and *caldo tlalpeño*. The Korean restaurants stayed open late and there were both expensive and cheap ones; all had truly delicious food.

In the Imaike district there were numerous *pachinko* or establishments with vertical pinball machines. The patron paid a modest sum in exchange for some little metal balls that he or she fed into the machine. If the balls entered into the right holes, the machine would spray dozens, hundreds, or thousands of little balls, whichever the case might be. The patron could exchange the little winning balls for cookies, chocolates, cigarettes, or other household goods. The *pachinko* was an emporium and an addiction for many. It was like making a bet because winning required strategy and luck, too. They said that the *pachinko* started in Nagoya. At first, the establishments were near the train and bus stations and working-class people were the ones who frequented them most. With the passage of time those businesses sprang up throughout the city and the passion for playing them became a craze for people of all classes. What's clear is that the *pachinko* stank of cigarette smoke besides the fact that they played music that, before long, burst your eardrums. On top of that, the machines were very noisy because different bells went off at the same time, just as the little balls entered the lucky holes. And to top it off, the light was blinding because each machine had at least ten colored bulbs that blinked on and off every two seconds, not to mention the almost phosphorescent and tacky colors of the machines. They looked like the kitschy dashboards on second-class buses.

No one could believe that in spite of this ambience, there were those who constantly frequented the *pachinko*. In fact, there weren't only addicts but also players who attended them religiously eight hours a day. The game became a way of beating life. They knew that if they spent eight hours seated in front of those machines, they could collect winnings equivalent to a day's pay. But it wasn't so surprising to see that addiction because *nintendō* games had just appeared and there was already talk about children and adults who spent hours in front of those screens. For everyone that was truly something new because we couldn't have conceived of it. It was a new era. Since the *pachinko* was and is a lucrative industry, when business seemed to be suffering, special days were launched with discounted hours for seniors and "families," although they were really for housewives.

They used to say that the *pachinko* was connected to the mafia because the latter controlled the gambling houses, the illegal establishments, the dirty, underground businesses. In fact, I once heard that in the past there were fights like in the film *Amores Perros*. It was also said that the owners of the *pachinko* were Koreans but the Koreans never admitted it. According to the Japanese, the Koreans were lying, trying to pass themselves off as business-people, when in reality, they were dedicated to "dirty business." Whether truth or lies, I don't know but the fact is that in the Imaike district there were many *yakiniku* restaurants, where we ate as we pleased, and the *pachinko* was the past-time of many people. There no one was discriminated against and even less so the clients since almost all were Japanese.

Sabetsu means discrimination. It's a word that's used very rarely. On the other hand, from what I myself saw and heard, there was segregation and resentment. Happily, after I left Japan, the situation improved for marginalized groups. Koreans now enjoy a better quality of life and there are new laws that protect their rights. Through good education and perseverance, they've acquired better positions. There are also personalities that have distinguished themselves in the world of sports and entertainment and there's also Korean-Japanese literature. On the other hand, when I visited Nagoya in 2002, something unexpected happened to me. Kimiko had already moved and was living in the eastern part of the city. I asked her to take me to the Central Park because I remembered it nostalgically. I told her that one of the photos I'd treasured most over the years was one I'd taken of that Borzoi. I'd even had it framed; I was wearing a light blue sweatshirt, jeans, and yellow shoes, what an outfit! But the most beautiful thing is that I was smiling from ear to ear. For years I cherished that photo because it reminded me of my happiest and saddest moments. When we were getting close to the park, Kimiko told me that she didn't want to take me there. But, "*doushite*—why not!?," I said, almost shouting. She remained quiet and grudgingly half-parked on a street some distance from the park. "It's that . . . the Central Park is full of poor people and beggars," she said as she bowed her head slowly. How?! It was true. The economy of the '90s had left many on the street. In those collapsing cardboard houses exposed to the weather lived the day-laborers because of lack of work and there were even people who'd lost everything because of their addiction to shopping. Without planning to, they'd gone into debt from their credit cards. It was a Japan that I never could have imagined. If it's now full of beggars, what will happen to the street dogs?, I asked myself.

Araceli with the borzoi in Central Park, 1982.

Karaoke
(Karaoke Music)

I went to a *karaoke* bar for the first time thanks to my friends An-chan and Miho-chan. I didn't know what a *karaoke* bar was and had no idea that people enjoyed themselves singing in bars with background music and a screen that displayed the lyrics. The *karaoke* machine was very big, about thirty by twenty-seven inches and it also weighed a lot. All that was a revelation to me. At that time, my Japanese was still at the baby stage but at least I could read one word or another projected on the screen. Although I didn't sing the first time I went to the *karaoke* bar and had no real style, at least I could recognize one song or another that was often heard on radio or TV.

Before I went to Japan, my Japanese friends in Mexico used to listen to a record by "Pedro and Capricious," a group from their country. They had a beautiful song, "Goban Gai no Marii e" or "Marie of Fifth Avenue." I listened to it so many times that I learned some of the lyrics without knowing what they meant:

> *Go ban gai e ittanaraba*
> *Marii no ie e iki.*
> *Donna kurashi shite irunoka mitekite hoshii.*
> *Go ban gai wa furui machi de*
> *mukashi kara no hito ga*
> *kitto sunde iruto omou tazunete hoshii.*
> *Marii to iu musumeto tooi mukashi ni kurashi*
> *kanashii omoi o saseta sore dake ga kigakari*
> *Go ban gai de uwasa o kiite*
> *moshimo yome ni itte*
> *imaga totemo shiawase nara yorazuni hoshii . . .*

71

Coincidentally, when I arrived in Japan the same thing almost happened to me because the hits were played everywhere. After listening to the same thing so often, you ended up repeating it although it might be just like a parrot does, without really understanding the song's message.

One of the first songs I learned was "Kaze tachinu" or "The Wind Blows," by Matsuda Seiko. Its melody was sweet and romantic, like the singer herself, a striking, elegant young woman. On the album-cover she wore a white dress and her hair almost reached her shoulders. She looked like an angel to us. Since she was only about eighteen, she'd barely begun her career, but her records were already selling in the millions. She appeared on all the TV programs that could book her; you could hear her songs on the radio every two or three hours; I'd go shopping and there was her voice again. In that atmosphere I began to memorize some of her songs. Without a doubt, the one I ended up liking best was "Kaze tachinu," which went more or less like this:

> *Kaze tachinu*
> *ima wa aki.*
> *Kyou kara watashi wa,*
> *kokoro no tabibito.*
> *Namida gao misetaku nakute.*
> *Sumire. Himawari. Furījia.*
> *Kougen no terasu de*
> *tegami kaze no inku de*
> *shitatamete imasu.*
> *Sayonara, sayonara, sayonara . . .*
> *Furimukeba irozuku sougen*
> *hitori de ikite yuke soune*
> *kubi ni maku akai bandana*
> *mou nakunayo to anata ga kureta.*
> *Sayonara, sayonara, sayonara . . .*

Everything happens backwards for me because first I memorized part of some song like this one and then I turned to the dictionary to look up words I didn't understand. Afterwards, if I still had doubts about any and had the chance to do so, I asked my pals for help.

The songs by Matsuda Seiko, or Seiko-chan, as her fans called her, were very tender. She sang about love and longing, and I completely identified with her. "The Wind Blows" goes like this:

When the wind blows
fall has come.
From here on in
my heart will roam.
I don't want you to see me weeping.
Better: violets, sunflowers, freesias.
From a balcony over a plain,
I pen these lines,
with ink on the wind.
Good-bye, good-bye, good-bye. . .
I turn around and see the field in bloom
feeling regret I could leave you to oblivion.
A red bandana around my neck—
the one you gave me when you said
"stop crying."
Good-bye, good-bye, good-bye. . . .

As soon as I more or less learned that song's lyrics in Japanese, I started singing it in the *karaoke* bar.

The great thing about displaying songs on the screen was that the lyrics were written two ways: as ideograms that were difficult because you had to study them for years, and in *hiragana*, a much more simplified and basic form that can be learned in a few weeks. So, when I was singing and suddenly the lyrics came to me, I'd turn toward the screen and read them the best I could. The Japanese, who were always kind at bottom, helped me read when they saw me struggling. Other singers, or rather songs, began to intrigue me, like that one by Itsuwa Mayumi:

"Koibito yo"

Kareha chiru yuugure wa
kuru hi no samusa o monogatari.
Ame ni kowareta benchi ni wa
ai o sasayaku uta mo nai.
Koibito yo, soba ni ite
kogoeru watashi no soba ni iteyo
soshite hitokoto
kono wakare banashi ga
joudan dayo to
waratte hoshii.
Jarimichi o kakeashi de

marason bito ga yukisugiru
maru de boukyaku nozomu youni
tomaru watashi o sasotteiru.,
Koibito yo sayonara
kisetsu wa megutte kuru kedo
ano hi no futariyo no nagareboshi
hikatte wa kieru mujyou no yume yo.
Koibito yo soba ni ite
kogoru watashi no soba ni iteyo
soshite hitokoto
kono wakare banashi ga
joudan dayo to
waratte hoshii.

"Lover of Mine"

When leaves fall in the dark
they know the cold won't be far
and on a bench moldy from rain
there's no one to sing me a love refrain.
Lover of mine, stay by my side
now that I feel the freezing cold
I want you to smile
tell me our parting
is a foolish thing.
I see a jogger
along the cobblestones
who seems to be telling me
    "forget him, everything is over."
I'm finally telling you good-bye, my lover,
seasons are turning,
we were a falling star
extinguished at nightfall. There's nothing left to do.
Lover of mine, stay by my side
I want you to smile
to tell me our parting
is a foolish thing.

The song begins with a slow rhythm and the singer's gentle voice, then it changes when she asks her lover to stay. Then her quivering, resounding voice accompanied by a series of intense notes makes you feel a pang in your heart. How moving to understand the language and enjoy the music!

It was an exciting moment because for the first time in history we could record programs. In fact, Kimiko and I learned how to use a video-recorder because we wanted to tape Michael Jackson's *Thriller*, which had been scheduled to air on TV. Without a doubt we felt moved to be living at a time when technology was changing everything. Suddenly not only was it easy to listen to music over and over but we could also watch our favorite stars until we got tired of them. I can't imagine *Thriller* without the performance that accompanied it. It was terrifying and fascinating to watch it over and over. Japan also had stars. Not of Michael Jackson's caliber but yes, stars. There was a pop singer, Kondo Masahiko, whom they called "Matchy." He was cool and I adored him. His song "Gin gira gin ni sarigenaku" was lively. It had a hundred-mile-an hour tempo and he danced as he sang it. He dressed in metallic colors wearing what looked like a space suit. Other times he wore black satin suits with gold and silver piping that made him dazzle. It was hard to learn the lyrics because I could barely make out the words. It was one of those songs in which the chorus got into your head and you repeated it in the bathtub, or on the way to the bus; but wherever you were going, its echo followed you. The refrain goes like this:

> *Gin gira gin ni sarigenaku*
> *futari no koi no yarikata.*
> *Gin gira gin ni sarigenaku*
> *sarigenaku ikiru dake sa.*
> *Gin gira gin ni sarigenaku*
> *soitsu ga ore no yarikata.*
> *Gin gira gin ni sarigenaku*
> *sarigenaku ikiru dake sa.*
> *Gin gira gin ni sarigenaku*
> *futari no koi no yarikata.*
> *Gin gira gin ni sarigenaku*
> *sarigenaku ikiru dake sa.*

"Softly Dazzling"

Softly dazzling
just like our loving.
Softly dazzling

softly we're nuzzling.
Softly dazzling
I simply don't worry.
Softly dazzling
softly I'm nuzzling.
  Softly dazzling
just like our loving.
Softly dazzling
softly we're nuzzling.

Of course the success of "Gin gira gin ni sarigenaku" had nothing to do with its lyrics or message but its rhythm. The song is long and isn't about much, like so many songs that manage to become the biggest hits.

Most of the *karaoke* bars were located downtown, in the Sakae district. It was strange because the Japanese used to build up or down. That is, while there were underground cities, bars were located inside tall buildings. There were eight- or nine-story structures that had up to 30 bars inside them. For me that was also something new. So, the customers knew about specific places because someone had told them or from high-powered publicity, typical in that country. It was common for *karaoke* bars to be located on a particular floor of a particular building. They always had stupendous service and served all kinds of refreshments and different kinds of snacks, although most people went there to sing along with the music. There were songs that I liked more for their lyrics than for their melodies, like "Sotsugyō shashin," by the composer, singer and pianist Matsutōya Yumi:

Kanashii koto ga aru to
hiraku kawa no hyōshi
sotsugyō shashin no ano hito wa
yasashii me wo shiteru.
Machi de mikaketa toki
nani mo ienakatta
sotsugyō shashin no omokage ga
sonomama datta kara.
Hitogomi ni nagasarete
kawatteyuku watashi wo
anata wa toki doki
tooku de shikatte.
Hanashi kakeru yō ni
yureru yanagi no shita wo

kayotta michi sae ima wa
mō densha kara miru dake.
Ano koro no ikikata wo
anata wa wasurenaide
anata wa watashi no
seishun sonomono.
Hitogomi ni nagasarete
kawatteyuku watashi wo
anata wa toki doki
tooku de shikatte.
Anata wa watashi no
seishun sonomono.

"Graduation Photo"

When I'm feeling down
I think of that album
and his photo on graduation
see his eyes; what fascination.
When I saw you in the street
my voice went mute
like in that photo, you were the same,
you hadn't changed.
Lost in the crowd
I saw my youth flee
sometimes from afar
I feel your reproach.
I hear a voice speaking to me
beneath the poplar in the breeze
and the road always taken
is only seen from a train.
Please don't discard
those memories we shared
you are
my youth.
Lost in the crowd
I saw my youth flee
sometimes from afar
I feel your reproach.
You are
my youth.

It was therapeutic to sing that song, which was so gentle, so slow, so sincere.

There was also a musical genre that was very Japanese and delightful to listen to. They called it *enka*. The songs were about homesickness, separation, melancholy, love and betrayal. They reminded me of our *ranchera* music. One song played often was "Ōsaka shigure," by Miyako Harumi:

Hitori de ikitekunante dekinai to
naite sugareba neon ga neon ga shimiru
Kita no shinchi wa omoide bakari
ame moyō yume mo nuremasu
Aaa . . . Ōsaka shigure

"Osaka Rain"

I can't keep living alone
Kita no shinchi, I miss you so
your neon lights drowned in my weeping
the rain has soaked even my dreams
Ahhh . . . Osaka rain

All the *enka* songs were like that, very sad and sentimental. I don't know why I liked that music so much. Maybe because it seemed so similar to our traditional music. *Enka* means spoken music and that's right because, as I understood it, it was a cross between a *corrido* and *ranchera* music. For some Japanese people, *enka* was music for the lower class. For others it was *Nihon no kokoro*, "the heart of Japan." I don't know, but what's clear is that that musical genre was born a little more than a hundred years ago and began as protest songs before it changed. Although, obviously, traditional music existed centuries before *enka* first appeared.

Karaoke, like so many other things, was an education for me. I never ended up using a *karaoke setto*, that is, a small almost-portable *karaoke* machine invented years later for home use. Suddenly many people began staying at home, no longer needing to go out to spend money in a bar. That was also a lifesaver for those who wanted to practice before embarrassing themselves in a *karaoke* bar. Now almost all the young people practice singing with a *karaoke* machine at school. What's amusing is that *karaoke* means "empty orchestra," although its function was and is to fill the emptiness in so many hearts. This may sound a little corny but *karaoke* is actually the voice of the Japanese people. Now that machine and that practice loved by so many people has been imported throughout Asia and, of course, to other parts of the world. Personally, for me, I liked *karaoke* bars because I could relax and learn Japanese there. As was to be expected, as soon as everyone found out I was Mexican, they asked me to sing "Bésame mucho," that immortal song by Consuelo Velázquez. They also asked me to sing, in Japanese, that lovely song of Roberto Cantoral's called "Tokei (Clock)." And on that note I bid farewell. I won't sing the lyrics because you must know them by heart:

"O clock, don't strike another hour . . . "

Katakori
(Stress)

You won't believe what I'm going to tell you, but this has to do with feeling sick, or nausea, to put it in medical terms. One Friday, I got up feeling like I wanted to throw up. I immediately thought about the meal I'd eaten the night before. I'd gone with my co-workers to the *robatayaki*. That is, I went like someone whose sole aim was to feed herself on pure vitamin T (yes, "T," as in taco). The *robatayaki* was one of my favorite places to eat and have a beer. That type of restaurant has a huge bar, usually in the shape of a horseshoe. The customers sit down and on the other side of the bar there's every kind of meat, fish, and vegetables; everything is raw. In the middle there's an enormous grill and whatever you order is cooked there. Everything is made on the coals using very little oil and the taste is delightful. It's as if you were eating . . . yes, in effect, grilled tacos, kebabs, *quesadillas* or something like those dishes. I thought that my mistake had been to go to that *robatayaki* where I stuffed myself on fish, pork, chicken, corn, and who knows how many other things. But Saturday arrived and Sunday, and Monday, and I still felt sick. That's when I decided to go to the doctor.

"I believe you're pregnant."

"But you haven't taken any test yet and I doubt it."

"That symptom of morning sickness usually means pregnancy."

"But, doctor. . . "

"Go home and return in 15 days, then we'll give you a pregnancy test."

And since in Japan you never argue with or question the doctor, like a little soldier, I marched home.

It wasn't the first time I went to the doctor. I'd gone previously when I came down with a strain of flu that I'd never had before in my life. I don't know why but at that time, getting the flu was so serious that it was common for the sick person not to go to school for up to ten days. At first, I thought people were exaggerating, above all because it was the first time I'd seen so many of them wearing face-masks on the street. It seemed ridiculous that anyone would walk around with a face-mask over his or her face; I'd never seen such a thing, only in local clinics where I was taken to be treated for hives that broke out from time to time. So when I saw people walking with face-masks on the street, I never thought that it was because they didn't want to be infected by or to infect everyone else. The fact is the flu was devastating for those who caught it. Did I say devastating? Now that I think about it, yes, that's right. With the flu came sore throats that had nothing to do with the tonsillitis I'd repeatedly suffered from. The fevers and aches I felt were also unfathomable. But I wasn't the only one, everybody else had the same symptoms.

The first time I went to the doctor was because I'd caught the flu. It was a real learning experience. You would be prescribed a medication and on the first floor you got the prescription. But instead of a pharmacy the place was more like a traditional drugstore where they prepared medicines the old fashioned way. That time, instead of capsules, they gave me powders and some little papers that looked like cellophane. It was assumed that I had to put the powders on the papers, pop them in my mouth and wash them down with a glass of water. What? Pop papers into my mouth? The idea seemed crazy but that's what the doctor prescribed so I had to do it. With complete *kimochi warui* (in other words, disgust!), I put the first paper and powders in my mouth and to my surprise, the paper dissolved immediately; the only thing I sensed were the powders, which felt like gravel over a wound as they went down my throat. But afterwards, let me say that they were a miracle cure, for a while. Oh, well, I had to stay in bed and stand that flu which for the Japanese was never serious but rather common.

The nausea continued and little by little I began to feel pains in my head and back. I returned to the doctor to prove him wrong about the pregnancy test. And so, he gave me his damned test and it was negative. And I didn't even complain to him, now you see, didn't I tell you? No, in Japan, as in Mexico, you can't confront your superiors. So I went home again. I'd heard that salted crackers were good for nausea. I ate them and nothing happened. I was told to drink cold water. I drank it and nothing happened. Of course, in

Japan, they treat everything with rice, just as in Mexico they treat everything with aloe and tortillas, even though the latter might be burnt on a wood fire so you can clean your teeth with some carbon smeared on your finger. I never had a problem eating plain rice with or without salt; my quarrel had more to do with eating the so-called *okayu*, that is, rice boiled to nothing. I'd never liked boiled rice, not even in Mexico when they put in tomatoes, potatoes, and sausage. In Japan it was boiled rice with a little bit of salt and that was it. For them it was the best remedy for the flu, nausea, diarrhea, and every other ailment. And, so they had me eating that *becha-becha gohan*, as Kimiko described *okayu*, which made me even more nauseous.

It seems as if your body tells you, wherever you go, you'll get sick like everyone there. I say this because I also broke out with the so-called *mizumushi*. So I agree. In Mexico I always suffered from skin ailments, maybe because mosquitoes used to leave me with boils the size of grapefruits or because I ate who knows what, and I broke out in a rash and then I was prescribed up to eight injections of penicillin. The *mizumushi* broke out on my toes. *Mizu* in Japanese means water and *mushi* means bug or insect. So the flesh between my toes began to crack, the skin split open, pus began to ooze out and walking became almost impossible. And then I went to the doctor again. "It's *mizumushi*, it must be treated with prescription medication and salves." What? What? The papers again? "No, pills this time . . . " Why were such strange things happening to me? Why were those water bugs popping out on my feet? Was it me or was it that all Japanese people suffered from the same things? That matter of learning the name of illnesses in a new language felt as if my body were also learning a new language and new ways of defending itself. I recovered from *mizumushi* when I learned that it was something more serious than athlete's foot; it was more like eczema. I also didn't know what eczema was because I'd never had it. So when it came to illnesses, I was illiterate in both languages.

My nausea continued and one day as I was complaining, my friend Mihoko came from behind and put her hands on my shoulders, as if to calm me down. Then she cried out: *kore wa katakori desuyo!* You have *katakori*. Exactly. It was like telling me, you have *mizumushi*.

"And that. . . what does it mean exactly?"

"Well, you have very stiff shoulders, like stone, like ice, like. . ."

"And who ever died from that?"

"Well, not died, no, but you're going to have to go somewhere to get a massage."

"A massage? I've always thought that was something just for men."

"You're crazy. Whether it's for men or women, they'll have to give you one to get rid of those knots in your shoulders."

Ok, ok. They sent me to nothing less than to a masseur who specialized in *shiatsu*. That is, a kind of massage that's done by using finger-pressure. It was strange because I'd never been given a massage before. I'd always associated massage with dirty or forbidden things. I remembered those ads in newspapers: "Beautiful masseuse. Young, blonde, sexy. Massage for gentlemen. Of all ages. . ." But according to my friend Mihoko, my ailment, my *katakori*, was the result of stress. She told me clearly: *anata wa suturesu ga tamatteiru*. Stress? Frankly, I'd never used the word stress in Spanish. It was for one of two reasons: either because I'd never been under stress or I was a foolish, innocent little thing (although it wasn't April Fools' Day yet) who didn't know that that word even existed in my own language.

The *sensei* or *shiatsu* masseur lived a few stops away on the subway and gave massages in his home. His wife was also a masseuse and the two took turns working. They didn't have special beds or anything else. He gave me a massage right there on the mattress, that is, the futon. He told me that he was the masseur for various *sumō* wrestlers when they stayed in Nagoya during the summer. He also told me he was in charge of giving massages to baseball players on the *Chunichi Dragons* team. It was true. I always fell into good hands thanks to my friendships. That's where I learned the meaning of a professional massage. It's called that not so much because the masseur was responsible for famous people, although I confess that as he massaged me, I imagined that those same hands had worked on that gorgeous Chiyo no Fuji, the wrestler, and on Hoshino Sen'ichi, the pitcher for *Chunichi*. It was more the fact that the massage was completely professional and was for many something necessary to stay healthy. *Shiatsu* would help my circulation because, according to the *sensei*, the ailments I had were the product of an obstruction in the flow of the "ki" or "chi." That is, the pressure from his fingertips would help my "ki" to flow. For me, all this was Chinese and with good reason. *Shiatsu*, joking aside, began in China and is related to acupuncture or acupressure. Masseurs focus on the so-called meridians of the body, that is, on certain parts of the body that are interconnected and where the "ki" flows.

No, you don't have to believe it but those massages through the so-callled "ki" can provide much relief. From the masseur I understood the intimate relationship between acupuncture and *shiatsu*. The Chinese have practiced acupuncture for more than 2,000 years and the Japanese, copycats in the end (although the Chinese don't sing *ranchera* songs too badly!), learned to cure themselves that way. I don't know if I ever understood the so-called meridians, but what I did understand was my acupuncture treatment, which I submitted myself to a day before going to the masseur. The mother of a dear friend had a heart condition and went every week to be treated by an acupuncturist close to Fujigaoka, one of the furthest-away subway stations. When she found out I was complaining all the time about being overweight, she encouraged me to go for an acupuncture treatment. No, don't think that they stuck in a needle and deflated me. No, no, it wasn't that easy. To begin with, I went to the clinic and had to wait on line because they didn't take appointments like when you went to healers or *santeros* over by San Cosme. The first time I waited and waited and finally went in to the *sensei*. He was a blind man. He really was blind. My friend's mother hadn't warned me, I suppose, so he wouldn't scare me. Would you trust a blind acupuncturist? No? Then ask those women how they can trust any old charlatan who gives them liposuction, or can drink any substance in order to become thinner without even consulting the list of ingredients. In my case, I was dealing with the man in charge of cases of real illness; so how could he not help me get thinner? Although I was actually not as heavy as I thought; it was just a product of my imagination.

When I entered his clinic, which was very dark, to be sure, he immediately sensed that I was a foreigner. He politely asked me my name and to sit down. And without asking me anything else, he told me he was going to take my pulse and instructed me to put my arm on a small pillow he had on his desk. After looking for my pulse a couple of times, he addressed me again:

Why have you come for a consultation?"

"I'm very overweight."

"Yes, but you're very healthy. Nothing is giving you pain and I don't think you have any problems with your digestion."

"I just get constipated a lot."

"You must eat a lot of rice and a lot of sugar, too."

"The truth is I do eat a lot. It's that I feel very hungry at night, at about ten, when I finish working."

"You're going to need to have a lot of patience."

"I will."

That's what I told him. I didn't dare to look at his face even knowing he was blind and couldn't see my pupils.

He put me on the bed and began to stick needles in my earlobes as well as in the outer ear. Then between my thumb and index finger as well as between my big toe and second toe. I asked myself what my ears, hands, and feet had to do with my excess weight if I'd never been fat in those parts of my body. I felt like telling him: no, the fat isn't there, it's on the other side. I continued going there a few more times, but since I was so young, I soon lost patience and I didn't give him the chance to help me with my desire to lose weight. It wasn't a lack of faith but a lack of patience. I was always impatient with things not related to studying.

On the other hand, when the masseur started working on my body, I understood why that acupuncturist stuck needles in the most unusual places. There was a connection between all the parts of the body; thus reflexology, or better put, massage of the soles of the feet, relaxes various parts of the body. In other words, reflexology doesn't cure but at least deals with reducing stress that's built up in the body. To put it in Chinese, it's about a correspondence or communication between the *ying* and the *yang*. The former is the feminine principle and the latter the masculine principle. That is, illnesses come from the imbalance of opposing forces and the treatment, whether with massage or needles, helps correct that imbalance and heals you and promotes the prevention of diseases. Explained this way, of course, I understood it. It's because of this that the needles are inserted in places that are far from the injured condition or let's say that instead of putting needles in my beloved belly, they put them in a different place.

My first treatment lasted two visits. The first day he gave me a full-body massage from head to foot. He kneaded me, concentrating on the places where he felt knots but only used his fingertips, applying pressure as he moved toward my head. I had knots mostly between my neck and scapulas and also in my hip. I didn't know what it was for until he worked on my heels, calves, thighs, hands, forearms and upper arms, and I felt the knots loosen. At the end of the first session, he told me to return two days later. When I arrived home after the first massage, I felt as if I'd been hit by a truck but I didn't feel too nauseous, and I was breathing better. It was as if I could also see things more clearly. In the next session, he gave me the same kind of massage but in the opposite direction; moving down, toward my feet. That was the only treatment I needed to cure my nausea and the stress I talked about before. "Come again when you feel under stress. It's the only way to cure it," he said.

The massage was expensive but I returned several times. I now understood that massage was essential to fight stress and illness. Well, you have to combine it with exercise, diet, rest, and other things. But, why did I have to go to Japan to find out that people become stressed out, and when it happens, knots appear in the body that cause uncomfortable symptoms and then diseases? Maybe it was the fact that in that country I was living as an adult for the first time? Or that stress in Mexico had another name that I hadn't known? How did people arrange their lives to get rid of their stress? Or is it that stress, or the so-called *katakori*, was something that only occurred in Japan?

I don't want to blame the Japanese but in their country they live under a lot of pressure. Well, at least that's how they lived at the beginning of the '80s. You always had to make a good impression on everyone: your boss, your neighbor, your teacher. You always had to do things with the group from your job or school and there was no way to escape. I remember one time, tired of coping with everything, I said I was very sick and couldn't go either to school or work. My lie made things worse. Suddenly people began knocking on the door and bringing me fruit or chocolates, freshly-baked bread. They didn't leave me alone day or night. All that caused stress I didn't know what to do with; and maybe it's true that I now brag using that word, which is already a common expression. I saw it in the house where I lived. Since Toshi-chan was a high-ranking manager, I told him, let's go to Acapulco for a week so you can play golf in Mexico under that wonderful Pacific sun and drink margaritas. "I can't because I only have five days of vacation." But you're a manager, I answered him. "Exactly, because I'm a manager, I can't create a bad example for my employees. I can't take more than a week's vacation." That's how the Japanese lived at that time, with a lot of money and few free days to be able to spend it.

They worked like beasts. And I was just one more. Because of that, I got along with them. On the other hand, so much work and so much pressure made me sick. They used to also get sick but they kept on fighting, they didn't stop, there was no god that could make them stop. For that same reason, I also ended up with my *katakori*. Still, at least I learned how to partly fight stress. *Shiatsu* became part of me, what I do to relieve exhaustion and stress. No, the Chinese don't know everything but what they've been doing for thousands of years are things essential for health. Because of that the Japanese have always learned the best from them. I did too.

Kaimono
(Shopping)

Imagine that Mexico City was heavily bombed and a group of architects had to redesign the city. Imagine the foreground of the scene, that instead of rebuilding the Cathedral, the government palace, shops, restaurants, and other businesses, it was decided to construct almost completely new buildings to be used as offices. Imagine that instead of the Templo Mayor, an underground city was built, one that ran from the Cathedral to the San Cosme subway, and in that city the only thing to do was go shopping or out to eat and nothing else. This half-terrifying scenario is more or less what happened to Nagoya after World War II. So, when I arrived in that city, its downtown was well-laid-out and neat with a few shops and restaurants that faced the street. During the day almost all the activity took place in Sakae, in the new underground city, or *Sakaechika*, as it was known. This city had entrances everywhere and long avenues that ran north, south, east and west. There were stores that sold all kinds of clothing, restaurants, cafeterias, bookstores, shoe-stores, candy stores, shops that specialized in kimonos, Japanese sweets, umbrellas, accessories, take-out food, cosmetics, and so many other things. Although the roof wasn't that high and the city was always packed with people, I didn't feel as claustrophobic there as in other closed spaces; maybe it was the bright décor and the fact that it had fountains and plenty of light.

As you went down to the underground city, it was easy to see that although it might be a beautiful day, people preferred to walk down below even when the stores weren't open yet. The habit of walking below and not above, on the sidewalk, had already been established. Besides, since there were so few display windows on the street level, the truth is that it wasn't so interesting. So, without even thinking about it, I also began walking all over the many underground streets every day. My God! Like a magic trick and without your really wanting it, they'd completely absorb you. It was as if in order to go somewhere you were forced to pass through the underground level of Plaza Satélite or Perisur or one of so many plazas that have cropped up in Mexico City. The music, the display of products, and the stores made you lose your head and you shopped like crazy, *kaimono* and *kaimono*, even if they were stupid things, still you bought them. I guess that this happens everywhere and not just in an underground Japanese city. Years later, I more or less had the same sensation when I walked along Avenida Juárez and it was full of street vendors. It's not that it was necessary to walk there but if it's the route that you're used to taking, and it runs toward the Eje Central, for example, what are you going to do? At least in Japan there were two choices: above, the streets were wide and quiet; below, there was noise, music, the sound of footsteps, roads, chaos, spending.

The service was so exceptional that you always felt spoiled. The sales-clerks never forced customers to buy, but they didn't ignore them either. They always looked out of the corner of their eye or gently, their gaze lowered, so that you didn't feel intimidated. I remember going into a handbag-shop and looking at one made of green suede; it was lovely, lined with turquoise-colored satin. It looked so expensive that I didn't even ask how much it cost and I left. Two weeks later I still kept wondering about it and I decided to return to see it again. When I asked about the price the salesman told me: "Well, let's put it this way, that's the purse you saw a few weeks ago and the fact that you've returned means that. . ." "I like it," I said without thinking. I was surprised by his attentiveness and that wasn't the only time it had happened to me. On another occasion, I also went to look at a coffee-colored leather bag whose price was beyond my budget. The salesman realized how wonderful it was and with that sixth sense that good sales-people have began to lecture me, explaining why it was sometimes necessary to buy things that were high quality. He told me that it was worth the investment because a bag is used every day. "And every day you want to feel good and look good. So, you can plan a budget and pay for things that are really worth it for you." He also told me something that only years later I heard come out of the mouth of someone who loved me very much: "If you don't buy good, expensive things for yourself, you may die and no one else will have bought them for you." If the salesman was indeed making use of sales-tricks, it was also obvious that through the time and patience he invested in me, he was a true professional. Most sales-clerks in that type of store didn't earn a commission; they had a fixed salary, but even so, their attention to the customer was something really exceptional.

Okyakusama wa kamisama desu (*The customer is God*), as Minami Haruo, an *enka* singer, used to say. That was the philosophy of anyone who served customers. But wait just a minute. Did that happen only in Japan? And in Mexico . . . was or is the service really so bad? I honestly believe that in Mexico the service is and always has been excellent but above all that happens in places where tips are given; and more or less in other places. In Japan, on the other hand, the service is always impeccable, even if people don't receive either a tip or a commission. Something else that's important is that over the last fifty years in Japan, the salaries have been quite good and in Mexico that's not the case.

But let me continue: the service in the department stores always impressed me very much. In Nagoya there were three of them: Matsuzakaya, Maruei, and Mitsukoshi. They were buildings right there, in Sakae, and each had at least six floors, besides a huge ground floor that connected to the underground city. So, you could enter those stores on the ground floor, that is, at street-level, or through the underground level. In the lobby of the ground floor there were benches so customers could sit or wait for their family-members and friends or simply for older people to rest. Next came the information booth, usually staffed by two guides dressed in impeccable uniforms consisting of a jacket and a pleated skirt, a white blouse, white gloves and a cap that matched the suit. All the employees dressed in uniforms close to those of the guides, but without a cap. In the information booth, there were free shopping bags for any customers who needed them, a telephone to make emergency calls, umbrellas, scissors, floor-plans, event-listings, free raffle tickets, special promotions for that day, and a world of other information. Further along, almost always on the ground floor, were shops selling perfume, accessories, and jewelry. There were two elevators operated by one or two female guides. When you got to the elevator, a guide was already waiting there and bowing. When the elevator arrived and it was time to get in, another guide was already waiting inside to receive you, stopping at every floor as she explained which departments were on each and the special offers there.

The guides' voices fascinated me and I imitated what they said, word for word, to myself. When I repeated them later to my

Japanese pals, they broke out laughing because, according to them, I imitated the guides perfectly. Japanese is like Spanish, even worse. The language is hierarchical; it doesn't just have the "tú" and "usted" forms but other hierarchical levels, as well as complexities and idiosyncracies that make a language very difficult, even for native speakers. So, when they heard me imitate a cultured form of Japanese, one used with customers in the store, it was a real scream. As soon as you got to the elevators, the guide used to bow, saying something like the following: "*Thank you for your cordial visit. Today and always we are deeply grateful to you. The elevator is about to arrive, it's arriving, it's just arrived. This elevator is going up. Many thanks for your visit.*" And then another bow. Once you were inside the elevator, the other guide began: "*Welcome. This elevator is going up. We thank you for taking the time to come to our store. We're going to stop at the first floor where you* (if not to say *Your Majesty*) *will be able to find ladies' clothing, shoes, and men's clothing. Today we have a such-and-such percent discount on such-and-such brands and we remind you that on the fifth floor we also have special deals. The elevator is about to stop. Let me open the door. We hope that you find what you're looking for and that you have a nice day. Many thanks.*" I ended up hearing that so many times that it was easy to memorize.

When you chose not to take the elevator, the voices possessed you anyway. You would hear this and that sweet voice coming out of the speakers and giving thanks for shopping in the store, thanking you for coming on a rainy or hot day, carefully explaining the cultural events to take place in the store, mentioning the discounts in different departments, explaining which seasonal fruits or foods were being offered, pointing out the possible danger of the escalator . . . Then in a different tone of voice, addressing the children: "*Hey you, young man, young lady, are you listening? Are you listening? Don't play on the escalator because you might hurt yourself. Before going up or down on the escalator, be sure that you're holding the hand of your mom, dad, or another adult. Don't run in the corridors because you might trip.*" Then it continued: "*Valued customers: we're honored to tell you and remind you that our baseball team, the Chunichi Dragons, won yesterday. To congratulate and honor them, we're offering you a 20% discount on such a day next week. There will also be a free raffle that will award 10 tickets to see them when they play such and such a team.*" Even though all this was good service and promotion, for me it was a learning experience.

The restaurants inside the department stores were also strange. There were as many as three or five of them with big windows that faced the street and there were cafeterias, too. I was told that this model had been copied from English stores, but since I didn't know England, it was all the same to me. Department stores weren't only places for buying things but also for culture. In general, on the top floor there was a space for special exhibitions where painters, sculptors, and experts in floral arrangement exhibited their work. So the public often went just to look at art. Not having much to do, I ended up losing myself contemplating the art in those shows. At first I didn't understand the painters' use of space. That is, I felt surprised seeing paintings that had so much white space on the one hand, and such small figures or landscapes on the other. Especially since I was used to seeing paintings and murals where the artist covered the whole canvas and wall. I thought a lot about Diego Rivera's "Dream of a Sunday Afternoon in the Alameda Central," which I'd surely seen once before going up to the disco at the Hotel del Prado, and about the murals in the Palacio de Bellas Artes, and the paintings of Orozco and Siqueiros that I'd seen in museums. Those painters never left any space blank. With time I learned that for Japanese painters, white space is as important as the people, objects, or landscapes that they paint. It was very difficult to understand then but I do much better now. I also managed to see exhibitions of floral arrangements which displayed masterpieces with gorgeous flowers, each well-presented in some exquisite vase. These floral arrangements were often accompanied by paintings of landscapes on screens with golden backgrounds. The beauty of that was understanding the relation between painting and floral arranging, which was nothing less than the representation of nature, art, and life. That's how I spent my time: seeing without understanding much of what I was seeing; admiring without being able to translate it all to my spirit; revering with the respect and love that we Mexicans have for art. In Matsuzakaya, aside from exhibitions, there was a small cultural institute where you could take mini-courses on the tea ceremony, flower arranging, painting, and calligraphy.

Another thing that never stopped impressing me were the basements of these stores. On the one hand, they were supermarkets, on the other, gourmet stores where you could buy exquisite imported food and also local seasonal fruits and vegetables. They also sold hot take-out food and there were candy shops, bakeries, and pastry shops that even had their own cafeterias right there. There were vendors in every corridor offering samples of food, drink, pastries, and bread. The neatness of those basements was amazing; you didn't feel as if you were in a basement but in a luxury store with flower arrangements wherever you looked and food and fruit arranged by wise, artistic hands like those of vendors in the San Juan Market.

The stores were never full of merchandise. They always were sure to have enough on hand so that the customer could buy without feeling pressured. On the other hand, there was certainly an enormous amount of personal attention there. But what caught my eye were the dressing rooms. They always had a silk, satin, or chiffon bag on hand for the ladies to pull on over their heads when they tried on clothes. The purpose of the bag was to avoid stains from makeup or lipstick on the clothes. And in the dressing-rooms there were high heels, at least two pairs, so you could measure the hems of clothes with them on, if necessary.

When an item was purchased, let's say a handkerchief, the sales-clerk would take it out with both hands, giving thanks and bowing. He or she would take off the price-tag and show it to you. Then, using a calculator that was huge, he or she entered the price and showed that to you to be sure there hadn't been any misunderstanding about what you were going to pay. In those kind of places, money was never received with the hands; instead the sales-clerk passed a little tray for the customer to deposit it there. He or she was always sure to state the amount being received. On the same tray the clerk returned the change and the receipt. Then he or she wrapped the handkerchief slowly and carefully and, instead of tape, stuck on a label with the name of the store on it. Finally, the sales-clerk would come out from behind the counter to deliver the item to the customer and offer more bows. In many places, sales-people shared a cashier who was in charge of receiving payments. That way, the sales-clerks were dedicated to wrapping the purchased items while the cashiers processed payments quickly. There were rarely lines because the system was very efficient.

Even though banks weren't shops, you would pay indirectly for extraordinary service there. At the entrance to the bank, there was always a person whose job was to direct the public. So that when you entered the establishment you didn't lose time looking for the right window. In banks, you never waited standing up; there were always chairs and seats and everything was managed automatically. It was 1982 and the banks already had televisions with big screens so that the customers could watch TV while they waited. Besides that, they almost always gave away boxes of disposable Kleenex. I always asked myself why banks in Mexico didn't learn from this kind of service;

well, not as far as offering things as gifts, but at least they could have adopted some of those ideas. I don't know up to what point banks were competing with post offices because the latter used to function like banks and their services were also skilled and polished. Besides, there were post offices everywhere. What's clear is that the service to customers in those places was as good as when you went shopping.

There's no doubt that service in Japan was a real delight although I'll never stop feeling guilty over something that happened to me. It turned out that one day I bought a pair of white trousers, very expensive ones, in fact. The first time I washed them, I decided to use bleach. Since I'd never used bleach before in Japan, without reading the instructions, I poured a few capfuls into the basin and left them to soak. When I took out the trousers, they were almost completely ruined. I started crying and Kimiko told me: "We're going to complain right now." We left. When we arrived at the store, the employee there apologized I don't know how many times. He took out a new pair of trousers, wrapped them up and handed them to me. Besides that, he gave me a light-yellow t-shirt, one of those then in style. We returned home and I felt delighted. When the day came to wash the new pair of trousers he'd given me and I was at the point of pouring in bleach, I made myself read the instructions carefully. Then I realized that the last time I'd poured in much more bleach than I should have. Feeling ashamed of my unfairness, I kept quiet and didn't tell Kimiko what had really happened. Surely she already knew since her female intuition never failed her. I could bet that the sales-clerk also knew but didn't want to contradict me because in the end, *okyakusama wa kamisama desu*. . . .

Nagoya's wide avenues near *Sakaechika*, 1981.

Akai Toyota
(Red Toyota)

It wasn't the first time I'd gotten into a red Toyota but that night, that car changed my life. Well, at least for a while. As it turned out, Kimiko had a Mercedes that always stood out on the street because it was a foreign car. Of course, there was more than one of them in Nagoya and the Japanese who drove cars made in their own country did whatever they could to avoid getting close to us. I don't know if it was out of fear of damaging the Mercedes and ending up with a catastrophic debt or a way of paying respect to the fat cat who drove that car. What's for sure is that whoever drove a Mercedes was rich; although being rich didn't mean you were a fat cat, or let's say, honest; you could very well be a *yakuza*, as they called the Japanese mafia. But it felt nice to ride in a cream-colored Mercedes. From there the world seemed different. In fact one of the things that surprised me most when I arrived in Japan was that cars had steering wheels on the right side. Therefore, the roads were also left-handed and confusing. I was used to seeing waves of *vochos* in Mexico City and as I crossed the street, my head was automatically programmed to turn to one side before I crossed. But in Japan, I had to get used to looking toward the other side because the cars came from the opposite direction. Well, at least that's how it seemed to me. Kimiko drove on the left side of the car, like they do in Mexico. Many foreign luxury cars had their steering wheels on the left side as well. I used to sit on her right, like when you get into a car in Mexico, but the traffic didn't flow to the Mercedes' rhythm because the drivers of those other cars were traveling on the right side of the road. I didn't know how to drive, although at one time or another my brother Cani had secretly let me drive my father's car on the soccer field when there weren't any games. Because of this, I became an expert at changing gears with my right hand. The drivers of Japanese cars had to change gears with their left hands and that always seemed very strange to me. Since I never drove in Japan, I never knew how difficult or easy it was.

One day Kimiko had to take her Mercedes in for repairs. They gave her a red Toyota so she wouldn't be without a car. In Japan, it seemed as if everyone owned a Toyota, but what impressed me was that almost everyone liked to have white cars. At that time, I thought that it was an incredibly boring color. What I didn't know was that the Japanese used to buy white cars (although now they buy silver ones) in order to resell them easily in three or four years. In Mexico, I never paid attention to the colors of cars, maybe because I lived there and didn't realize certain things or because we Mexicans don't like to do things the same way as others. The fact is that an *akai*, or red, Toyota wasn't an exceptional car, although of course, I was happy that it was red and not white. It was Sunday night and we were returning home. Our friend Mihoko was riding with us. I don't remember if she was sitting behind me or Kimiko. Suddenly I felt as if someone were smashing a plate into my face. When I opened my eyes, the Toyota had crashed into a gasoline pump. I looked behind me and realized that a car, a white one, to be sure, had plowed into us and ended up embedded against a streetlamp, right there across the street. I saw two tires rolling along the road but there was no sign of the driver. I don't know if it was my Mexican instincts or if my head was simply conditioned by my bad experiences but the first thing that occurred to me was that that car, the one to blame for our misfortune, was about to escape. The shock didn't let me react and realize that without tires, that car wasn't going anywhere. Then I got out of the Toyota and ran toward the white car to take a look. A man was stretched out, face-down. He's dead! I thought. I began to shout for help as I began distancing myself, without realizing that I was walking alone in the middle of the road. People began coming out of buildings and approaching me. Suddenly I remembered that Kimiko and Mihoko had been with me and I returned to the red Toyota. The ambulance arrived in a few minutes and loaded the three of us in. That's when I realized that my right knee was bleeding. They immediately took X-rays and the doctor ordered me to stay in the hospital wearing an orthopedic collar because the impact had been very strong. This will be a matter of days, I thought. It wasn't so. And for some reason that I still don't understand, accident victims must be brought to the nearest hospital, even if it means taking an elderly person to a pediatric hospital. They moved us to Marumo Byōin, a hospital that specialized in cancer, where they mostly treated women. Kimiko and Mihoko were lucky but I had to stay there a couple of months.

Gan means cancer in Japanese. You learn that word very quickly in Japan. They used to speak a lot about cancer there, or so it seemed to me. There had never been cancer in my family, which made that whole experience very strange for me. At first they put me in a room with a little girl on whom they'd performed who knows what kind of surgery. I never figured it out. Before her operation, we became fast friends and it surprised me how quickly she recovered. I was injured in the back and that horrible thing they put around my neck made me feel as if my head were about to explode. I had to remain lying down almost all day but my hands were free. I don't know if it was some kind of spell or what, but I soon began to embroider. The mother of Okada Yuki, the little girl, began to bring me skeins of wool and frames already set up that were easy to baste. The patterns were simple and I embroidered them with large stitches, as I always did, in my own style, always very slapdash. Thanks to my mother, I'd learned to embroider when I was nine years old. And that's how I began spending my days, embroidering and talking until I got tired.

What I never figured out was why the patients had to pick up their own meals. The staff carried the meals on trays and left them there, just like that, in the hallways. We all ate the same thing. It was tasteless, boring food that I never got used to. I also had to get up myself for my meals, whether I liked it or not. The only time the nurse brought a patient meals was when he or she clearly couldn't get up. When I went for my meals, I found myself around the cancer patients. Almost all of them had gone through surgery, or so it seemed. When I got tired of being in bed and went to walk through the hallways, I also found them. They walked very slowly and carried I-V's of saline solution or catheters or both. I saw them doing slow exercises and could see from their faces that they were in soul-wrenching pain. Their sad but hopeful pupils said everything. Little by little I learned the language; whether someone was being treated for stomach, uterine, breast, esophogal, or lung cancer. I never spoke with patients directly about where they'd been operated on. Words weren't necessary. If only they had been! It was well known that for years and years, after World War II, about 60,000 people died from cancer each year. And at the beginning of the '80s, the high mortality rate from cancer made it the main cause of death in Japan, surpassing heart disease. It's estimated that the statistic reached 200,000 people when I was in the hospital.

I'd seen sick people in my life but the pain experienced by these patients was something that couldn't be explained. How terribly sad. "Your stay in the hospital is making you sicker," my friend Yoshitake Keiki told me over the phone. But the doctors kept me there and there I was. Not all the patients complained equally. There was a sweet little old lady, very sweet, who got excited when she saw me embroidering. One night she approached me and asked if I wanted to practice making *origami* with her. The Japanese have an enviable relationship with paper. I thought that in Mexico we were inventive because our artisans used to make true works of art with *amate* paper and even as children we'd make planes, ships, and caps with any paper on hand. And when it got close to December, we would begin to decorate *piñatas*. We would paste strips of newspaper firmly all over the clay pot. Then we would cut and curl tissue or vellum paper into shapes of carrots, onions, and even stars. On other occasions we would become adventurous and with scissors we'd cut holes in pieces of folded tissue paper. Although those folds were never as beautiful as real Mexican perforated paper, at least we had fun. In Japan, *origami* was something different. The paper itself already came stamped with exquisite shades of red, white, purple, and blue. Many had fans or willow leaves printed on them. The paper looked like a piece of silk from a kimono although of course, it was much thicker.

I began making *origami* shapes. My clumsy, impatient hands folded the paper very badly. That's when I realized why I'd failed my geometry classes. My ungrateful memory won't let me remember that little old lady's name. I only recall that she came from a family of writers. She was highly educated and seemed to be very rich. The truth is that cancer doesn't forgive anyone. She made *origami* cranes in every color. I observed there that various patients had necklaces of white cranes hanging on their headboards. They explained to me that since long ago it was believed that when someone makes 1000 *origami* cranes, (a tradition known as *sembazuru*), a wish will be granted to him or her; like when you hope for something and promise to fulfill a vow. That seemed beautiful to me because of the few wishes and vows that I knew of; one was crawling on your knees along the whole Calzada de Guadalupe or entering it that way through the entire atrium of the Basilica on the 12 of December. One day a couple visited me with their eight-year-old daughter and the little girl brought me a complicated *origami* figure as a gift. It looked like a geometric sphere with innumerable sides. It makes me shiver to think of the time it took her to make it. To make and remake it. In *origami*, many times the piece gets ruined and you have to start all over again. But what an act of generosity. How can it be that we Mexicans only know how to give thanks with food. Only to us would it occur to give sugar or chocolate skulls on the Day of the Dead. As if for us, what isn't eaten can't be known or felt.

The days passed. They sent Yuki home and moved me to a common room with nine other patients. That's when I really felt that I was in a hospital. Everyone would cry at all hours of the day and night and it became harder and harder to get sleep. I began to walk more slowly, like them, as if I wanted, whether I liked it or not, to be part of their life, their rhythm. I began to get depressed despite the fact that I had my life in my hands. I would walk dragging my feet along that passageway which seemed interminable. At the end, to my left, were the stairs and to my right a small waiting room with coffee-colored chairs. There were never visitors or patients in that forgotten corner. Through the window I'd see the street and the pedestrian walkway. Across from that was the Matsuzakaya Sutoa. From above you could see the red awning with white letters and a parking lot on the second level. Outside Matsuzakaya Sutoa, taxis were parked in their stand, almost always five or six of them. To one side of the taxi stand was the bus-stop and further on you could see the Hongo subway station. Every day, hallway, Matsuzakaya Sutoa, parking lot, taxi-stand, bus-stop, subway station. . . . hallway, Matsuzakaya Sutoa, parking lot, taxi-stand, bus-stop, subway station. The whole time I stayed in the hospital, Kimiko only came to visit me once. I never reproached her. I don't feel what people call rancor. Maybe for that reason I was lucky because every day, every day, including days of celebration and religious holidays, I was visited by my friends Ronda Atkins and Clifford Meyer, the American couple who gave me such affection and hope. They were professors of English. Clifford taught at Nanzan University and Ronda also taught, at another private university. As we said good-bye, already late in the afternoon, I would notice the sun hiding away and the glow of some firefly. Then as night came on, I always felt uncomfortable again.

The head nurse used to see me and feel sorry for me; for that reason, she decided to change my room but it wasn't for the better but for the worse. This time I ended up sharing a room with a patient who cried all the time. I don't know how old she was. Maybe forty. She'd already lost all her hair. She would kneel on the floor or on the bed, doubled over. When she didn't have her face pressed against her legs, she would cry with her head sunk into the sheets and then she would chew on them, scratching them with her weak nails. She begged with cries but not words. Seeing her suffer so much, I ended up asking myself whether she was begging God for life or death. What a petty and horrible thought. . . . but it was only because I'd never seen anyone suffer so much. I began to confuse day and night. I didn't care. She didn't sleep because of the pain and I couldn't shut my eyes because of depression. We were two zombies in the hands of whatever might give us life. Death didn't dare visit us.

As far as my back, I don't know if it was an act of God but little by little the pain was diminishing. The truth is that in the hospital they weren't doing anything, they just kept me there in bed, wearing an orthopedic collar. My head began filling with strange thoughts. I began to count the number of tiles in the room, then the hallway. I saw that sad blue color, close to gray, even in my dreams. Then I ventured further and began to go down the stairs. Our room was on the fourth floor and at first I only could go down one floor. It was very difficult walking after so many days in bed. So, I stopped to rest every two or three steps. I went about studying the three pencil drawings in wood frames. They weren't signed but they seemed to be by the same artist. The first showed a white woman without any Japanese features with a tail and a striped dress with long sleeves. She was seated with laced fingers and a vacant expression on her face. The second woman was looking in the same direction, to her right, and had short blonde hair; her eyes somewhat slanted. She wore a nightgown that looked like a uniform. Her arms were completely out of proportion because they were too wide and long. Her fingers were also laced. The third image was disturbing. The woman sat uncomfortably with her hands under her legs. Her dress was disheveled; it looked like someone had pulled on it. Her face was pure suffering, although you couldn't see her eyes clearly; her sparse hair was tangled. She looked like she'd lost a lot of it.

The next week I went down to the second floor. The pieces there were reproductions of paintings by Robert Thom on the history of medicine. They had scenes of women attended by doctors. I well remember one of a black woman kneeling on a table, dressed in blue with a red head-scarf. Before her was a doctor in a black suit, like Abraham Lincoln, and two assistant doctors with gray jackets and trousers. Below it said: J. Marion Sims. Another painting showed a doctor examining a patient's eyes. The woman was elegantly dressed with a long, ruffled dress. Below it said: Hermann Helmholtz. Finally, the next week I walked from the second to the first floor but didn't go completely down; I stopped three steps short. There the pieces changed drastically. They were happy scenes of women and landscapes in reds, greens, oranges, and purples, almost surreal, like those that sometimes illustrate children's books. From the third step I saw to my right the "Beaver Tea Salon," although it was deserted. Outside, near the hallway, there was a vending machine for drinks and to the left a flower shop with the same name as the "Salon."

My roommate continued feeling bad but kept confronting life with all her strength. I ended up being a coward. I was cowed by that life. I begged the doctor to release me from the hospital, under any conditions. I told him that I didn't understand why they had me there just resting and going crazy. Ronda and Clifford agreed. Besides that, they used to say terrible things about Japanese hospitals: "Look no further! What's the good of so much money and technology if medically, they're so backward? Have you seen how old their equipment is? This place looks like a prison, not a hospital. When has anyone seen patients having to pick up their own meals? What the hell is this, a self-service store or what? The Japanese need to learn from American medicine and hospitals. In the United States, hospitals are modern, neat, and professional!" They never got tired of criticizing them. They ate them alive. Since I only knew hospitals in Mexico and one or another clinic in particular, I had no way to compare. When Ronda and Clifford saw that I couldn't take it anymore, they demanded a 48-hour pass for me from the doctor. They wanted to prove to him that I could be at home without medical assistance for 24 hours a day. They took me to their apartment near the Issha subway station. There they took care of me and fed me soups and imported American food.

I left the hospital on a Thursday afternoon. It was a beautiful October day. When I went out to the street and stepped onto the sidewalk without any support from anyone, I felt as if the ground were moving beneath me. I'd just been born. I had to learn to walk again. In a little while, I found out that the young man we'd collided with was speeding at almost a hundred miles per hour, completely drunk, and his car insurance had expired. The Japanese laws were very strict concerning each one of those three violations. That poor Christian, as people up north would say, had committed all three. Not only had he lost his license for life but he was in jail paying for his offense. On top of that, he also had to pay for the physical and material damages. It seems that he lost everything, even his house. When I learned about this complete disgrace, I thought a lot about what my father did when a freight truck ran over my grandmother and cut her in two. I was five years old and when they came to inform us about the accident, we all ran to the place where it had happened. My grandmother was completely covered with a white blanket. In the distance we saw one of her sneakers; with that we realized how far the truck had dragged her. The driver had escaped and when they caught him, my father said that he forgave him: "What good would it do me for them to put him in jail and for that poor soul to let his family be abandoned if that won't bring back my mother to me?"

I never got into a red Toyota again. It wasn't fatalism. It just wasn't written in my destiny. Well, at least not up until now.

Buta Mitai
("You Look Like a Pig")

"*Buta mitai.*"

"What did he just say to you?"

"Nothing."

"What do you mean, nothing? If that's true, why do you look so surprised?"

"Forget it. It's nothing."

"Then why are you so red in the face if it's nothing?"

"It's that Japanese people. . . ."

"What did he say to you? Tell me."

"He told me that I look like a pig."

"What a lack of respect! And from a chiropractor! I'm telling you, that's why I never learned Japanese. Because it's better not to understand their filthy talk."

Ronda was right. The chiropractor or, to put it in Japanese, a specialist in chiropractic, was the one who insulted me at the end of my first appointment. As friendly as the Japanese were, they also had their weak points. All my life I'd fought against being overweight. Note that I said overweight, not obese. I was one of those typical girls and adolescents who liked to eat a lot. At fifteen, I wasn't allowed to eat sugar and I was submitted to a strict diet which made me lose 25 pounds. After that, I had my ups and downs, my slips, and then my weight would go up again. As a girl I suffered insults. They laughed at me in school, calling me "Moby Dick." But all that was dead and buried. So the last thing I wanted to hear in Japanese was *buta mitai*, you look like a pig.

I was hurting but not in the mood to confront Japanese people, above all, respected individuals. I never was like that. That was my Mexican side, which seemed so much like them. I wanted to be open and frank like my American friends, but I just couldn't. Many times I'd heard coming out of the mouths of Japanese people: "you're very fat although, of course, your legs are slim and your face is, too." Why did they have to meddle so much into people's bodies? What also clarified things for me was that they never used their hands to express themselves but when it had to do with my weight, they raised them and made an imaginary circle as if I wouldn't understand the meaning of *futottieru*, you're fat, or simply, *buta mitai*. It was nothing like the *piropos* you'd hear in Mexico.

"Sink yourself into all that flesh. . ."

"With a chubby girl and a little *pulque* . . ."

"All that meat won't let you sleep. . ."

But if I was fat in the eyes of Japanese people, it surprised me that in spite of being so slender, Japanese girls had such fat legs, besides being bowed. I ended up having that conversation with them not to insult them but because the proportion of their bodies seemed so strange to me. They told me that their legs became bowed because of the way that they kneeled on *tatami* mats, sitting on their calves. I never questioned their theory because the truth is that sitting the way Asians do is agony. My legs always fell asleep, I always felt uncomfortable, I even ended up feeling pain inside the part of my body that makes people with hemorrhoids suffer so much. Although I took classes to learn how not to feel so tired, that never stopped being a torment for me.

"*Hige haeteru.*"

"*Sō desune . . .*"

That was the other thing. They never stopped reminding me I had a mustache. That was one of the other biggest complexes of my life. And I don't know if it was a curse but soon after I arrived in Japan, my mustache grew thicker and, to top it off, darker. The panic of having to shave and the thought of my skin becoming rough, like a man's, upset me. At that time I hadn't used or heard about hair-bleaching creams so I had to accept what I was and that was that. At home no one had excess hair so I didn't grow up with a culture of hair removal by waxing and didn't even knew that there was an alternative. If it had occurred to me to ask the handsome gay guys I admired so much when we went to see their show, it would have been different. But no. It wasn't lack of hygiene or slovenliness but innocence and awkwardness. One day I had myself made up in a cosmetics shop and the first thing they did was completely shave my face. That's when I discovered that lots of Japanese women shave their entire faces, except their eyebrows, so the fuzz doesn't ruin their makeup or face-powder. They had an obsession with whiteness, above all their faces, that's why my mustache, although they never told me so, must have made my face look dirty. The discussions were never-ending about powders, creams, or makeup that they took off or covered spots with. I realized how much they spent on makeup to cover the obvious blemishes from the sun. At that time they paid up to 30,000 yen. In cash. Of course. They barely went out in the sun and many women did so wearing rain-bonnets or wide-brimmed sun-hats and white gloves. They couldn't stand freckles even on their hands. For them it was something horrific.

They also used parasols from early on in the morning. They preferred fabrics in pastel shades. They almost always were highly decorated, edged with lace. The handle, the ribbing, and the rings were delicately worked, too. Those women looked like they'd stepped out of the movie *Mary Poppins*. Before returning to Japan the second time, I went to Puerto Angel for a week. It was December and taking advantage of the incredible weather and the beauty of the Pacific, I got completely tanned. Or better yet, I baked myself under that radiant sun, facing that surging sea and horizon worthy of a thousand postcards. Who cared? At that time no one talked about skin cancer. Or maybe I was too young to worry myself about those things. So when I arrived in Japan I felt as if I were in a circus because far from celebrating my tan, people said to me "you're very black." Nothing like "sun-tanned princess" or "black beauty, where did you go?" No. That's when it hit me. They were frightened by blemishes, freckles, by anything dark or black. Coming from a country with such a wealth of Indian, white, black, Asian, and mestizo cultures, the issue of color had never even entered my head. I was so used to seeing blacks in Acapulco and in Veracruz, Indians everywhere, from Chihuahua to Yucatán, Indians even in my own house and in my own lineage, blondes in the north and so many Chinese in restaurants, that for me the idea of a race and a color was something as alien as Mars.

I have to admit that when it came to my eyes, they were always tossing me compliments. *Me ga ōkī! Me ga kirei!* Such big, beautiful eyes! *Matsuge ga nagai!* Such long lashes! The truth is that in Mexico my eyes weren't anything out of this world but for them they were as grand as the sun. They longed to have been born with narrow eyelids and round eyes. The plastic surgery craze had begun but it cost a fortune. As far as that, famous artists and models were the ones who appeared on TV with rounded eyes and brown or blonde hair. They were what Japan simply was not. Just like in Mexico, it's enough to watch TV and realize that almost everyone on-screen is blonde. As if we Mexicans were all blonde and blue-eyed. The other thing that the Japanese had a complex about was the size of their faces and the truth is that in comparison to the svelteness of their bodies, their faces were very big. When I lived in Japan, Japanese people were still short and slender. They ate very little meat and a lot of fish and this was reflected in the size of their bodies. After I left Japan, the diet there changed, and young people began growing very tall, like never before in their history, except for some divers and native fishermen from some islands where they always were tall and, like it or not, very dark. My nose was something else they admired. They told me that I had a "*takai*," or "long" one, that is, the opposite of short. With all that, I spent so much time thinking about my face and my body that I don't know if it was my anxiety about it or if I ate too much rice and too few vegetables or what but I became horribly constipated.

The reason why I went to see the chiropractor, or expert in chiropractic, is because I still had a lot of back pain after my accident. I didn't like either his treatment or much less his baby-talk. So Ronda advised me to see an expert in *kyu*, or what they call moxibustion. It was all Greek to me because I didn't understand what moxibustion was, either in Japanese or in Spanish, but I agreed to go. The doctor spoke impeccable English but that did me little good because I could speak to him in his own language. The first thing he said was that I was overweight. Here we go again! Then I learned that in fact, back pain could be the result of bad posture, or that having large breasts could also cause it. But neither of those applied to me so it was obvious that I was in bad shape from the accident. I didn't know that the doctor was going to touch the same spots on me as the *shiatsu* masseuse and acupuncturist did. His treatment wasn't massage but some chiropractic-type exercises and later he burned my skin with *mokusa*, that is, with a small cone that held the root of a mugwort plant. It was like someone approaching your body with a lit cigarette and letting the ashes fall on you. The treatment didn't hurt at all because they put some small pieces of gauze around the area to be burned. The only thing I didn't like was that they left me with some black spots on my body that lasted a long time. I suppose that moxibustion would have eased my pain and helped restore balance to my body. But going to that doctor was a torture, not so much because of the burning, but because of what he used to say about my excess weight. I explained to him that I was suffering from extreme constipation. "Then you must eat at the same time every day." I did that and nothing happened. The only thing that finally cured my stomach long afterward was a bitter Chinese herb that I drank. The worst part of it was that instead of constipation, it gave me diarrhea. To be honest, I didn't like the *kyu* treatment. There's nothing like *shiatsu* and it's not necessary to be pricked with needles or burned. Eventually, the pain went away and I stopped my treatments and having to experience what for me were insults.

Although I wasn't even twenty-two, I'd already noticed some gray hairs. That was something else: "You have gray hairs showing." And was that my fault? Besides, my family wasn't at all gray-haired, so I didn't have to worry. Hair for Japanese people is sacred and it's believed that you have to take care of and beautify it all the time. One day I was walking down the street and was surprised to see a shop window with men's wigs. They were made for bald men and not for those who wished to just change their hairstyle. There were all kinds there—ones with a fringe, with sideburns, with a part on the left or on the right, ones with curly, wavy or straight hair, with classic and modern cuts and styles. What didn't they have! I suppose that no one likes to be bald but for Japanese people, it was obvious that it repulsed them. The men took great care of their hair. They went punctually to the barber-shop or to the unisex hair salon. They were treated so well that I even felt jealous. First the stylist would wash the customer's hair very gently and slowly. Then he or she would cut it with incredible care, as if making a sculpture. The stylist was sure to use every kind of scissors, from normal ones to special scissors for thinning out the hair. Then the customer reclined and with a little pair of scissors, the stylist snipped off the hairs that had accumulated inside the nose. The next step was applying the shaving cream. And, as if caressing velvet, the stylist would glide the razor over the man's face to be sure that no nib of stubble remained. But that wasn't all. He was then given a five-minute massage and the wax was removed from his ears with a long bamboo stalk. Those men ended up looking like gods!

Going to the Japanese hair salon wasn't only a necessity but an expense. You paid for the service, for the neatness, for the design of the salon that they'd decorated with elegant curtains, flower arrangements and exotic plants. They almost never lacked tea or coffee. And the stylists were experts who'd studied and trained under the strict supervision of their teachers and colleagues. There were plenty of magazines displaying the latest haircuts. So that each stylist felt the need to have lots of old and new examples for the client to choose from, according to his or her taste. Those Japanese magazines circulated not only in Japan but also in other places in Asia such as Hong Kong, Taipei, Kuala Lumpur, Singapore, and, above all, Seoul. In that environment, you felt almost compelled to get a good haircut. Although many Japanese women opted for the classic cut, which consisted of a fringe and straight hair to the shoulders or halfway down the back, they had it cut and straightened regularly so it looked like a curtain of black silk. Hair had always been a priority, even in ancient times, when men as well as women had long hair and tied it into pony-tails and into elaborate hairstyles that they adorned with gorgeous multicolored bands. The women used combs, hairpins, and clips made of tortoise-shell and other exquisite materials. But in the '80s, only actors who performed on old programs wore wigs that, since they were artificial, looked bad. I soon realized that *sumō* wrestlers were the only ones who had well-coiffed long hair.

Going to the hair salon was like attending a special event. I felt important because of the way I was treated there. First the tea or coffee, then the magazines. After that, the assistant washed my hair and gave me a delightful massage on my scalp and at my temples. Before she was done, she was sure to also massage my shoulders. The ritual of haircutting began with different kinds of scissors. When the hairstylist was finished, he dried and then combed my hair. But the experience didn't end there. He would look me over from the front, back and sides, and send me back to his assistant to have my hair washed again. Again? Yes, again. The whole time, the assistant stood behind the stylist as if she were a bodyguard or statue and observed step by step what he was doing. The assistant was the one who rinsed my hair another time, dried it and led me back to the chair. The stylist cut the final strands of hair, those only he himself or an eagle would see. Finally the straightening or the hairstyle that I'd wanted began. It cost an arm and a leg but the service was worth it; besides, going out in style really had no price. At that time, the latest style meant shaving one side of your head and leaving the other side with long hair; a style very punk, very English, and also very much à la Cindy Lauper. That's how they cut my hair and I enjoyed it immensely.

Only once, in another salon, did the stylist cut and straighten my hair into a typical Japanese look; that is, she cut it very straight with a fringe and falling down in back to my shoulders. It was the first time that I wore a kimono and my hair had to be in tune with my outfit. Not every stylist is up to the task of cutting or styling the hair of women wearing kimonos. Those hairstyles are very elaborate and incorporate hairclips or combs that must be coordinated with the color of the kimono, the purse, the sandals, and above all with the occasion because kimonos are for special events. It's very common for the stylist to also be an expert in *kitsuke*, the art of kimono-dressing, an ancient art that of course is not at all easy because it takes years to learn. Since many women don't want to ruin their hairstyle, they bring the kimono to the hair-stylist so that she herself styles and dresses them. In my case, first I went to the stylist and then I was dressed at home. How I suffered! I could barely walk because I felt my sandals chafing the skin between my toes. To top it off, you can't walk quickly, out of lack of habit and because the kimono is stuck to your body. It's for that reason that when you see Japanese women in kimonos on TV or in films, they seem to be walking with the grace of a fairy godmother. What people don't understand is that walking quickly is practically impossible. That rose- and pearl-colored kimono squeezed me too much, above all my stomach, and I could barely breathe. Finally, the day I put it on, I could barely eat because I felt that the *obi* or sash was bursting my belly open. What a pity. I was hungry. There's no doubt that she who's born shaped like a *tamal* . . . But even with all that, even with all the lard packed into those delicious tamales, it wasn't necessary or fair that one day I would be called *buta mitai*.

Waratte Iitomo
("It's OK to Laugh")

I answered purely out of politeness. The truth is that it didn't even enter my head that a gray machine fifteen by six inches could record things. That's how I was presented with the first video recorder I'd ever seen. It had cost nothing less than 200,000 yen in 1981; that is, something like two thousand dollars today. Little by little, we learned how it worked and in the course of a year, used it only about two or three times, no more. We just weren't used to recording programs and watching them afterwards. That's how we lived then, learning about new things all the time. I remember that one of the gifts I treasured most was a *walkman*, the first that came out from Sony that year, model WM-2. It was gray, very heavy and had a blue leather case and enormous headphones with orange sponge-padding. I was told that it had cost a fortune. Of course it had. In Japan, such devices were always expensive and we felt the need to keep up to date. It was all about being in fashion. To have old equipment was embarrassing. So, people did everything possible to be at the height of technology. I got scared when I learned that the first automatic electric cooking-pot for making rice had been launched by Toshiba in 1955. With so many years on the market, the electric rice-cooker that we'd been using had advanced by centuries. People put the rice in at night and programmed it for the hour they wanted the following day. Then the rice cooked by itself and stayed hot in the pot for hours. For me, all that was progress without limits.

TV was a window into Japanese life. In Mexico I never watched TV in the morning. I don't know if it was because we were always in a hurry or because there weren't programs that caught our attention or because we were used to listening to the radio. The thing is that Japanese programs hooked you. From early in the morning they had correspondents in all parts of the country reporting the weather and speaking about the newspaper headlines, as well as cooking and other programs. It was enough to watch them only a couple of times to become addicted, even if at first you understood very little. Since the images helped me to understand, I felt transfixed watching them displayed on the screen and repeating what was said. Most of the time the programs were presented by two people so it was easy to understand because they spoke to each other. After the excitement of the morning shows, the samurai programs began. These were what I liked least because their dialogue seemed incomprehensible and I always hated to see characters wearing fake-looking wigs. But I couldn't complain since at the same time or afterwards, educational programs would come on, English lessons at beginning and intermediate levels. Since I knew little English, I watched them because they were highly entertaining. The presenter would take some book and read from it as images out of the story appeared. Then the sentences were reviewed and there were pronunciation exercises, and finally a quiz. I adored those programs. I waited for them anxiously. I never thought about it seriously but years later I realized that I'd learned a lot of English through Japanese. And why or how did I understand Japanese grammar? I didn't know it. I'd learned it purely by intuition. I'd leafed through a book I had. That's how I studied the language, repeating words hundreds of times until I memorized them. I repeated without questioning and thought only in Japanese. At that time, my life was very uncomplicated because I barely knew the language and couldn't worry too much about anything. My environment was very limited and although I never thought of it this way, with less, you learn more. Life is easier if you don't think too much.

Since there was a TV craze, there were screens in snack-shops, bars, and restaurants; something that wasn't done in Mexico at that time. The peak hour for programming was, surprisingly, twelve noon on the dot; right when people went out to eat. I'd been used to waiting anxiously for the programs at night in Mexico; when we watched *Rich People Also Weep* and other telenovelas that were so popular then, but I wasn't used to watching them during the day. In Japan, to help distribution, screens were installed everywhere, in the lobbies of buildings, and next to billboards on the street so pedestrians didn't lose even a moment of the most important programs. That was a wonder to behold. Aside from important news-reports, at noon the most popular programs came on.

There was a variety show called *Waratte iitomo*, or "It's OK to Laugh," which from the beginning was hosted by the extraordinary comedian Tamori (Morita Kazuyoshi). The program aired live every day, from Monday to Friday, and an enthusiastic audience attended in the Television Fuji studio in Tokyo. The comedian came out singing *"How do you do?" "Gokigen ikaga. . . ."* Then he sat down to talk with a guest celebrity. Clever and amusing, he always asked questions that stumped or confused the guests or said things that made them laugh. At the very end of the program, the guest called a famous friend on the phone, generally someone known by the audience, and the conversation was broadcast live. It was then that the guest was asked whether he or she wanted to be on the program and the guest had to say *iitomo*, which in this case meant *yes, it's worth it* or *absolutely.* And the conversation continued like that. Sometimes, to break the routine, he invited other fascinating comedians, like *Sanma* (Akashiya Sanma), or all kinds of contests were organized and there were sure to be auditions or trials. That's how the show attracted all kinds of people, with or without talent, but everyone had an opportunity if not to appear on the program, at least to go through the experience of having been put through the test.

"How is it that you can understand the Japanese on *Waratte iitomo?*"

"I don't know but I do. It's my favorite program and Tamori fascinates me."

"But what I can't get into my head is how you manage to get his humor."

"I don't know. I never thought about it. I only know that one lucky day I sat down to watch the program and I understood it. I started laughing at the silly things they were saying and from that point on, I was addicted."

"If you understand Tamori, then you don't need to study Japanese."

"Of course I do because even if I understand almost everything, I need to learn the cultured form of Japanese."

"Cultured Japanese my foot! Language is everyday speech and nothing else."

I had never-ending conversations with foreigners who attended the Japanese language school where I ended up studying.

As a loyal fanatic of the program, I became a *fan* of Tamori and my dream was to get to meet him one day. I dreamed of going to Tokyo and personally introducing myself to tell him how much I admired his talent. If at that time, I'd shown his photo to someone Mexican, he or she would have asked me, "Who is that guy with the face of a pickpocket?" He combed his hair straight back with Vaseline and always wore very dark glasses. He wore polo-style shirts. And v-necked sweaters. His favorite color was sky-blue. After watching him on TV so much, one day I realized that he had a problem in one of his eyes because the lid drooped; or maybe that's how it looked to me. That was the reason for such dark glasses. So, at first sight, this man wasn't anything special, it was like seeing some Mario Moreno in the street without knowing that that man was Cantinflas; a guy like so many other Mexicans, like so many other Japanese, all too common.

One day, out of lack of imagination or who knows what, the show began with a segment on hearty eaters, if not to say gluttons. In effect, it was a competition between two people who ate something and the winner received a prize. When it was announced that they wanted contestants to eat cookies there, I saw my chance. The next week, I took a bus and headed for Tokyo. To avoid paying a monstrous amount for a hotel, I traveled at night. Soon, I saw the bus approach. I got on sweating and coughing but my cough wouldn't stop. People around me began to get worried, above all because the trip is six hours and surely they were asking themselves if I was going to keep on like that all night. They asked me if I needed some kind of medicine.

"No, I'm alright. I think it's just nerves. In a few hours I'll be standing on line to see if I can appear on *Waratte iitomo*. . . ."

They kept looking at me with those eyes of seeing but not believing. They didn't answer at all. And after a while, "mmmm, I hope you feel better."

The bus arrived at four in the morning and I waited in the chill of dawn and took the earliest subway to Shinjyuku station. When I arrived, there was already a line of dozens of women who obviously had stayed awake longer than I had. In my cherry-colored bag I had some bread and cheese, apple juice in a disposable container, and a small bottle of Sangre de Toro in case I felt nervous. The Alta Fuji TV Studios were in a building in the Shinjyuku district. When the line began to move, my legs wobbled and I felt as if I were falling. What would happen if I couldn't speak? If in a moment of terror, Japanese were erased from my mind? Or if I fainted? The line moved quickly. The studio staff were asking people their age and God knows what else. I suppose that they were experts in judging a person's appearance, charisma, and brilliance. With one or two questions, they could size up a contestant's diction and speed of response. That was the first trial. I'd purposely worn one of those ponchos from Chiconcuac, made of wool and embroidered cross-stitch. As soon as they realized I was a foreigner, they sent me to the second round. The most important thing was creating a sensation. They wanted something different. The second trial was easy: they made us eat in pairs and of course, in the end, the ones they chose would appear on TV that day.

That time, they chose a strange young girl named Osanai Takako. Tall, white, very white, earnest, quick, and with a great sense of humor. She was dressed in the latest style. She wore a blue jacket, a white blouse with an impeccable collar and a long, gray skirt. Her hair, short and asymmetrical, was half-punk, half-strange. To top it off, she was a maid, a position which little was known about and above all was never discussed. That was the best thing about that program. It gave everyone the same opportunity and if the organizers saw someone with talent, they recruited him or her if not for that program then for others. The producers were incredibly sharp. It was 8:45 a.m. when they informed us that they'd made a selection. So we had to rehearse the segment. The referee was going to be a famous TV sports announcer. But before practicing, they submitted each of us to an hour-and-a-half interview. She was in one room, I was in another. I suppose that they needed to know as much as possible about the contestants. The grilling was such that they even asked me if I had dogs or cats and what their names were and other such things. Then the moment of the rehearsal arrived and we sat down to compete eating cookies, each at her own little table; I was to the right and she was to the left of the announcer.

As we rehearsed, in the midst of all those bright lights from the television cameras, I noticed that there were people seated in the studio audience. I looked again, more attentively, because I had the feeling that someone well-known was there. I looked even more closely and realized that right there, before my eyes, was Tamori. He was smoking and instead of an ashtray he had a green plastic pail where he tossed the ashes. He was seriously concentrating as we rehearsed. I couldn't believe my eyes. He was smaller than he looked on TV. I also couldn't believe that he could be so serious. I felt as if someone had unmasked me, exposing me and making me see reality. Or the opposite, as if someone had unmasked *him* and I suddenly discovered that there was an ordinary man behind that idol. I say this lightly now but at the time I felt betrayed.

The show began at twelve noon. I was put in a closed room, alone. When it was time, the staff came for me and I introduced myself nervously but with a big smile, ready for anything. The referee began to ask me questions and told me that he'd visited Mexico several times to watch wrestling at the Toreo. "Oh! Close to my house," I told him. "It's such a small world. But why the hell have we begun such a personal conversation?," he said. It was all a big laugh. Suddenly he introduced the sponsor, that is, the owner of the company that would be donating the cookies we were going to eat. He was a black American, tall, with a lot of personality. He was wearing a hat. Since I knew little about American culture, I didn't know that he was Wally Amos, the ex-agent of Simon & Garfunkel and now the owner of the world-renowned "Famous Amos Chocolate Chip Cookies." The competition began, we ate the cookies and I was the winner. They awarded me a medal and a box of cookies. It was a round can with the image of Wally Amos printed on it. Years later, as I learned, he began to write self-help books and all that, but when I was facing him and didn't know who he was, I acted spontaneously with him.

The program ended and although I didn't have time to talk with Tamori, I felt fulfilled. We said goodbye, I went down the elevator and already an enormous crowd was below, waiting for those of us who'd just appeared on TV. At the entrance of the building there was a giant screen so that interested people, gossips, and others who didn't have anything else to do could watch. Not just that, but it was in one of the most famous places in Tokyo, a spot where hundreds of people met each other to go out to eat or take a stroll. As I got off the elevator, a couple who'd traveled with me on the bus the night before were waiting for me. They'd been curious and parked themselves in front of the screen to see if the crazy girl who'd taken the bus with them the night before was really going to appear on TV. They invited me out to eat but I told them no. I felt overwhelmed and besides had made plans to visit the house of a Kabuki performer whom I'd met at the Bellas Artes theater in Mexico City. I walked throughout the city and people recognized me in the street. How could they not when I was dressed in such folkloric clothes that looked desperate for attention? I was a young girl and without thinking about it that way, I felt proud to have finally seen Tamori in the flesh. I took a taxi and the driver said to me: "You looked very good on TV. Congratulations." I turned red and didn't know how to answer. I felt my heart swell unexpectedly.

The next day I left Tokyo. I took the *Shinkansen* and people recognized me in the train. It felt great. When I arrived home, they'd already called me from Fuji Television. They wanted me to return to the program. This time they would cover my train-fare and give me 10,000 yen for my participation in the segment they'd be presenting—foreigners who would respond to some Japanese expressions by drawing pictures. I felt luckier than ever. I returned to Tokyo the next month, bursting with pride, and excited about participating again. That time I did introduce myself to Tamori and he immediately told me, "I remember you, you're the cookie-girl," and continued smoking. Since they knew me at the studio, I could watch the beginning of the program from backstage and didn't have to wait in a closed room. I saw how between commercials, as Tamori stepped off the set, at least three people were waiting for him. One awaited him with a lit cigarette and put it between his lips while the other wiped the sweat from his face and the third removed the microphone. Wow! What a life, so hectic and frenetic, and yet so dull, without smiles or anything!

Our segment began. I came out with two Americans. One was blonde and fat, very fat. The other was rail-thin and tall, very tall. We answered the questions that Tamori asked us with jokes and laughter. The skinny girl won the contest and all was well; the program ended and each of us left on her own. When we got to the street, everyone recognized me again. This time I was tired, very tired because I'd spent a lot of energy. I would have liked to have been snappier but I couldn't. I suppose that when you don't do things naturally, they simply don't come out the way you expect them to. So I didn't succeed as a comedian. Even less as a performer. I got to meet the great Japanese comedian and saw his nervousness and flaws first-hand. He wasn't how I'd imagined him or maybe it's that when your dreams become reality, everything changes. I suppose that's it. I lived a few minutes of fame and returned to my day-to-day life—boring and at times, even simple. But thanks to Tamori and his *Waratte iitomo*, I kept laughing every day.

With Wally Amos at Fuji TV Studios
after the *Waratte Iitomo* show, 1984.

Osanai Takako, who
appeared with Araceli in
Waratte Iitomo at Fuji TV
Studios, 1984.

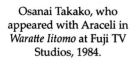

Araceli (center) on live
TV with Tamori (Morita
Kazuyoshi), 1984.

Ikebana
(Flower Arranging)

The factory and its offices were located in a city with the same name: Toyota. It was a new city, like many others. Or, better put, it had been a small town called Koromo but after the war, when the automobile industry was booming, it became a city that grew by leaps and bounds, especially in those years of such great prosperity. But I didn't go to the city of Toyota because of cars; I used to go there because that's where my teacher of *ikebana*, or the art of flower arranging, lived.

I would take the Meitetsu, that is, a train that traveled to the outskirts of Nagoya. I'd arrive in about forty minutes; it was like going from Mexico City to Toluca. The school was near the train station. It was a house with an enormous living room and a stone floor, rectangular tables and a large sink for preparing the flowers. The classes were held at different times. I'd go in the morning and my classmates were ladies in their thirties or older. I knew that in the afternoon, the classes were filled with young women my age, but I never felt uncomfortable in my morning group. My teacher, Tanimura Kouho, was nothing less than a teacher's teacher, or an *iemoto*, as they were called. She was charismatic, pretty, and elegant. The first thing she told me when she introduced herself was that she came from Kobe, a sophisticated city south of Osaka, known for its architecture and Western tastes. From that point on, she never got tired of repeating that in Kobe, people knew how to dress well and had refined palates. "In Nagoya, on the other hand, people don't know how to eat. They put too much salt and seasoning on everything. Besides that, the noodles are hard and the portions enormous. What crude tastes these people 'these people' have!" Since she was my teacher, I listened and kept quiet although I felt secretly pleased that *these people* liked generous portions and well-seasoned food.

Through practice, I began to learn the art of flower arranging. For the first lesson, my teacher brought in materials that I'd need, and sold me everything except the vase. There were lots of oval, triangular, square, rectangular, and asymmetrical vases in that room. . . . So I bought flowers, a pretty pink plastic bag to carry them, *hana basami,* or scissors to cut the stems, and a *kenzan. Kenzan* means mountain of swords but actually it's a small metal base three by two inches. On its surface there are thick spikes where the stems are stuck to keep them strong and erect. The *kenzan* is placed inside the vase so it isn't obvious that that's what holds up the flowers.

The first thing I learned is that only three flowers are necessary to make a perfect arrangement.

"In other countries dozens of flowers are used, they're tied together and placed in the vase, but not here. Here three are enough."

I also learned to cut the stem diagonally.

"Pay attention: the stem is always cut inside the water and even better if it comes from the tap or another source of running water. The water can't be cold or it will chill the flowers. Be sure about that. Otherwise, the flowers won't last long."

Other basics in my training included finding the most attractive side of the flower.

"Flowers have many faces. Hold one by the stem and turn it slowly. As you'll see, the flower's appearance changes depending on how you turn it. When you find the most ideal side, that flower will look lovely, appearing in all its splendor. You will feel as if it were moving; you will feel it breathing."

I don't know if it was just my age but it's clear I'd never paid any attention to flowers; I'd never even received a bouquet. My mother, on the other hand, loved flowers. She'd grown up in a house with a big patio that was arrayed with colors. She could name all the flowers. How I thought of her during my first lesson! For me, it was all a new language and experience, although I have to admit that I seemed to be hearing an echo of her voice when she used to say "you must speak to plants." In Japan it was the opposite: Plants speak to you.

I made my first arrangement with violets that were a pale lilac hue. It was March. How lucky to have begun that month, when the colors of all the flowers are delightful, especially after a raw, icy winter. In order to make the lesson more agreeable, my teacher told me that one flower is supposed to be the father, the second the mother, and the last one, the child. The father would always be the tallest one, the mother of medium height, and the child the shortest. But cutting the flowers' stems according to their size and putting them on the *kenzan* and then in the vase wasn't enough. My teacher pointed out that for them to live together like good families do, I'd have to arrange them in a pleasant, harmonious way. So we spent the rest of the class arranging the flowers on the base. She made me fasten and remove them I don't know how many times as she kept repeating that the father's name is always *tai*, the mothers's *yo*, and the child's *tome*.

As the end of the class drew near, she gave me a little green book with the words *Mishoryu Gyokko* spelled out in artistic calligraphy, and depicted beneath them, her family emblem. The first twenty pages contained an introduction to *ikebana*. It was accompanied by diagrams, numbers, and geometric shapes. When I saw that, I got scared because I remembered my classes in geometry and all the angles as well as the horizontal, slanting, oblique, parallel, and diverging planes. My teacher realized immediately that drawing and what geniuses call "theory" weren't my strengths. "It's only a notebook bound with graph paper for you to illustrate the principles you'll be carrying out," she told me. In effect, it was a notebook or manual where I had to record the date, style, and materials, even the names of the flowers and leaves or branches we were using, if that were the case. Besides that, at the top of the grid-lined pages I had to draw the arrangement as it looked that day. At the end of class, she told me to put the flowers in the bag I'd bought and when I got home to practice what I'd learned over the next few days.

The next class was different. When I arrived, she served me green tea. "Always be sure to take the cup gently and slowly. Place it in your left palm, turn it a little toward you with your right hand and raise it to your lips. Don't look at me. Look at the tea, the cup, or at the floor but never look up because that's bad manners." When I started to sip the tea, she suddenly told me, "flowers must be arranged by the heart and spirit, not by one's hands." What she wanted to tell me was that any arrangement I made would reveal my deepest feelings because it's through flowers that your state of mind is revealed and the respect and affection you feel for others. How I thought of the flower vendors in the markets in Mexico!

In that second class, we returned to the same theme, *tai, yo, tome*: the father, the mother, the child, but this time using a kind of poppy. She explained to me the importance of arranging the flowers into a perfect form on the base. And I said, just to myself, *but why?* Why is it so important to arrange them so well if the base can't even be seen because it's always inside a vase that isn't transparent? Like it or not, during the rest of that class, my teacher explained to me that it was necessary for things to be perfect, above all when they weren't visible. It felt very strange to hear that in Japan what's not seen is what's most important. That day I also learned that Japanese women pay more attention to their undergarments than the clothes they put on to go out. That is, the care they give to their stockings, slips, corsets, or garters suggests their own self-respect. Then I realized why the seams that I'd made in design school had to be as perfect as the invisible stitches on the outside. But is it possible that only Japanese women were like that? It made me think about Mexican women, about their modesty, their impeccable cross-stitch embroidery. Anyway, what was definitely true was that the Japanese were obsessed with perfection. They also spoke about something called *kei-haku-tan-sho*, the principle of making things light, slender, short, and small. As is well known, they're geniuses when it comes to miniaturizing, but what was surprising was that even the tiniest things had to be perfect on the inside, too. That's where their success in designing and assembling calculators, radios, and computers comes from. There's no doubt that the philosophy of *kei-haku-tan-sho* is also reflected indirectly in the arts. An example of this is the bonsai, a tree that's deliberately manipulated to keep it small. Like all trees, the bonsai keeps growing but it's constantly clipped. That way, the tree can be kept outside or inside the house because it gives the impression that nature has been set in an inner space.

Classes continued and one day my teacher arrived with wildflowers that she'd cut from alongside the road. She said that she'd brought them on purpose because store-bought flowers were now too expensive. She wanted to show us how wonders could be worked with what's found in the fields. On that occasion, she informed us about the categories within *Mishoryu Gyokko* or the School of *Ikebana*, which we now belonged to. She told us there were five levels and that in the past all classes began with the first, known as *Seika*. But it was much more complicated now that there'd been a transformation so the masters decided to begin with *Moribana*, a simpler but highly appealing category because with two or three flowers you could fashion an elegant floral arrangement. She also explained to us that in the past the arrangements were made with only branches and wild plants, and that the latest trend was to return to the past and use those materials again. For that reason, that day she wanted to show us how the work of her ancestors could be repeated right there. That was one of the lessons I learned the most from because I began to appreciate nature differently. That day, with three cuttings from bushes and a single flower, we made beautiful arrangements. As we practiced making them, my teacher told us we could use different parts and types of bushes like the hyssop, stamens, pistils, elderberry buds, thorns, blossoms, holly and wild vines!

But what took me a long time to finally understand was the use of vessels. I'd always liked clay pots, including those made of black clay from Oaxaca, and of course, Talavera earthenware. Although I'd never stopped to ponder and study Mexican vessels, they had that special something that always attracted me, whether it was their colors or shapes. Maybe we Mexicans are born in love with our own art although few of us speak about it. In school, we used vases of all shapes, sizes, and colors. In *ikebana*, the receptacle is as important as the flowers because both must come together in perfect harmony. Little by little, I learned to cut flowers according to the size of the vase and to choose its color. You must assume that the receptacle represents the earth and the final floral arrangement should suggest a natural landscape with flowers planted in it. Before I realized that, I didn't understand my teacher's insistence on using dark-colored vessels—green, gray, coffee-colored, or almost black. On some occasions, she chose the vase and for us students, it was a challenge to arrange the flowers so they matched the vessel's form. Other times there was a lottery and we were obliged to use the vases that fate had bestowed on us. But I'm not complaining. More than once, my teacher generously gave me orange receptacles and it was a true delight to fill them with birds-of-paradise, daisies, or other flowers as vividly colored as I was used to.

"What's most basic is what's most difficult. That's the most complicated thing to learn." One day my teacher began the class with that affirmation. "In general, people believe that the basics are for fools and novices, but that's not true. When one finally understands the basics, it's because he or she is at the point of becoming a master." I couldn't believe what I was hearing. "Think about it. People are ashamed to ask basic questions because they're afraid they'll be considered common. But in reality, what's basic is the most challenging and difficult to understand." I remained thoughtful, just listening. By this time, I'd already realized that the *ikebana* classes weren't just classes in flower arranging but lessons about some aspect of life. At first, I didn't understand why we had to sit listening to such things before beginning to cut and arrange flowers. Besides that, it felt strange to be learning so much about life and nature in a city where cars were made.

I wrote to my mother to tell her that in Japan each month has its own flower. Well, at that time, it never even passed through my mind that it's the same everywhere. But it made me happy to tell her I'd learned that each flower had its own language, beginning with the month of January: the pine tree during that month meant longevity and the bamboo plant, virtue; the *trinitaria* in February represented memory, the orchid, an open heart, and the violet, chaste love; in April the cherry tree meant ideal beauty, the tulip, fascination, and so on. I wasn't hoping for it although I should have expected it: My mother answered me immediately, asking if in Japan, there was Burro's Ear, Bull's Blood, Bird's Claw, Macaw, bougainvillea, Cancer Grass, Virgin's Mantle, *ayatito*, Mexican olive, and only she and God knew what she was asking me. The letter sounded like a tongue-twister! In fact, when I read it, I remembered that when I was in grade school, they made us memorize "Izquixochitl Reina Xóchitl Moctezuma, Ilhuicamina, Cacamá." The oddest thing was becoming aware that the more I learned about Japan, the more I realized what I knew about my own culture.

But more than the arrangement and language of flowers, I learned some essential aspects of Japanese etiquette from my teacher. I knew that young Japanese women learned good manners at different stages of their lives, but I didn't expect that this would also happen in *ikebana* classes. On more than one occasion, the class lasted all day. We had to come in prepared to be dressed in kimonos by my teacher and other female assistants or owners of kimono shops who were thus experts in the art of kimono dressing. We began the day drinking tea. Afterwards the laborious work of putting on the garment got underway. Once we were impeccably dressed, the etiquette lesson began. They taught us how to greet someone when arriving at his or her home because in Japan there are various rules. Above all, I liked learning how to kneel, placing my hands on the floor and bending as if kissing it. It was an overly respectful rule but it fascinated me. I also learned how to deliver a gift because it's assumed that when you visit someone's home, you should never arrive empty-handed. Like in Mexico. Except that in Japan, you must be very careful with your hands when delivering and receiving gifts; they should move slowly and gracefully. There were blocks of *tatami* mats I learned to walk across without touching the divisions in-between. It was a blessing to learn how to sit so that my feet didn't fall asleep. And finally, we were taught how to drink tea like it's done in a formal ceremony. The ceremony is a complete ritual from the preparation to the way you sip the tea, which was very bitter, to be sure. In the end, being young and inexperienced, I respected the solemnity but what I liked best were the sweets that accompanied it. My teacher told us repeatedly that the purpose of the ceremony was to cultivate true inner peace; because of that her fundamental spirit could be expressed in four words: harmony, reverence, purity, and tranquility.

On other occasions, after our lesson, we spent time together in the same classroom or went to my teacher's home. That gave us the chance to learn something about cooking. My teacher was always ahead of schedule; she was the one who had to teach us how to cut vegetables and, above all, fruit. From her I learned to submerge the already-cut fruit and certain vegetables in salted water because they taste more delicious that way and don't turn brown. One day, as we were cooking, I told them about *flores de migajón*, the ornamental flowers made from breadcrumbs. They couldn't believe it until I explained to them, completely seriously, that the paste for those flowers is made with glycerine and glue. And to top it off, I also told them about the *calabaza* flower and how tasty it is when prepared in soups and *quesadillas*, with mushrooms. . . and about Aztec pudding. The next time we met to eat after class, I told them about *nopales*, how delicious they are and about their exquisite dahlias, *biznagas*, and jonquils that bloom in a unique color: Mexican pink.

Also, thanks to my teacher, we were able to go to Kobe to exhibit our floral arrangements in one of the salons of a famous hotel. In that very place, she introduced me to the great poet Kusumoto Kenkichi. I spent a whole day with him. The poet composed some *haiku* for me that I should have memorized because, in my innocence, I didn't realize that one day I would lose that yellowed paper where he'd written those sacred verses. I have only one photo of us together. I suppose that "a picture is worth a thousand words" but how can I recover the echoes of those almost holy moments?

In *ikebana*, nothing was easy. Nothing was made easy for me. So I assumed that I was barely learning the basics of a good education.

Araceli (second row, second from right) with her *ikebana* classmates; master teacher Tanimura Kouho (first row, second from right), 1984.

The author exhibiting her own flower arrangement, 1984.

Shitamachi
(Old Town)

When I returned to Japan for the second time, Kimiko had already moved to a neighborhood close to the Nagoya Castle. It was a very desirable area because of the amazing views of the castle and because it was the oldest part of the city. Very close to her condominium was the ultra-luxurious Nagoya Castle Hotel where top celebrities stayed. In the summer a group of us girls would go swimming in the hotel pool, although it was very expensive. They also sold drinks and two or three small dishes at very high prices. Because it was so close by, when the heat became truly unbearable, we used to spend afternoons there. What I hated the most, although I never said anything to anyone, was seeing mafioso types wading into the same pool we were using. I could recognize them from the enormous tattoos that covered their backs.

Tattoos had always disgusted me. As a girl the only tattoo I'd ever seen was the one worn by the sweet-potato vendor who used to pass through the street selling his wares. People said that he'd been a prisoner and those who never believed that story were convinced when some guys who ordered sweet potatoes from him barely escaped without paying. Right there he took out an icepick and chased them. He scared them so much that when he reached them, they started crying, and everybody felt sorry for them. In Japan it was common for mafiosos to get tattooed. It was said that tattooing was an old practice that emerged not with the mafiosos but with moneyed people who got tattooed on purpose to display their status. It was also a ritual. Since then artists (there really were tattoo artists) began to introduce different colors and pictorial designs on traditional themes. From the beginning, tattoos covered broad swaths of the body.

Tradition or not, it disgusted me to enter the pool knowing that a tattooed man had submerged in the same water . . . even if it had chlorine in it. I asked myself why such a luxurious hotel would allow those mafiosos to share the same space as everyone else. The truth is that the Japanese mafia was everywhere. It was easy to pick out its members even if you didn't see their tattoos. They wore very extravagant clothes but all of it in bad taste: white trousers and white shoes. In general they wore dark glasses and gold chains hung from their necks and wrists. Their watches were very flashy and as for their rings, don't even ask. Most of the time they drove the fanciest luxury cars, at times foreign models that were too expensive for most of the population.

The mafia didn't hide from anyone. They showed up wherever they felt like it. And ordinary people like me didn't dare look them in the eye. Wherever they were, they imposed their presence: being near them you'd feel a heaviness in the air charged with fear and threat. A friend of Kimiko's, an Afghan doctor, half bald and with a crooked nose, super-intelligent, although very annoying, told us some things about the mafia. The guy must have read everything and if not, only God knows where he got his information. His Japanese scared the Japanese themselves because he challenged them one after the other with new expressions and unknown words. He knew so much that my work colleagues and I used to laugh behind his back and asked ourselves if he himself weren't a *yakuza* or mafioso. He never wore anything different from outdated suits of coffee-colored velvet, and to top it off, he drove a red Mercedes. In the end, Mangel, the doctor, explained to us that the mafia had been around for more than two hundred years and that it was truly an institution in the full sense of the word.

It wasn't a secret. There were films, plays, and even short stories about the mafia. In fact mafia members published (and still publish) their own magazines and even made alliances with political parties. I remember how one of its big-shots said on TV one day, "If we don't give work to the prostitutes, peons, bricklayers, ex-convicts, idiots and fools, who will?" With an air of grandeur, he insisted that the mafia took care of all those people whom society rejected. He also said that they provided people with what they wanted most, even if the government prohibited it. It was known that the mafia controlled drugs, shady loan- and betting-joints, houses of prostitution, and large chunks of the construction and entertainment industries. This was known, although of course, no one ever saw how they carried out their operations.

It was horrible to listen to stories about the mafia and being confronted with their tattoos was like a curse. They say that in the old days, tattoos fell out of fashion among well-off people. Then they began to be given only to criminals to identify them. In fact, the more offenses they committed, the more tattoos they were marked with, and they were tattooed on the face and arms so it would be obvious. Later, tattoos made a comeback and prostitutes from the old Edo (Tokyo) and Osaka had the names of their favorite clients tattooed on their arms or thighs. If discretion were preferred by these women or men (there were also men who were prostitutes), they just put a series of dots with a number signifying the customer or lover's age. Ironically, Buddhist monks and nuns also began to get tattooed. It was said that it was a way of expressing their connection with Buddha. Tattooing was completely banned for an entire age but decades later it had another revival and became so fashionable that everyone began to get tattoos. The mafiosos wanted to distinguish themselves from the rest of the population and began to ask for extensive tattoos that covered their backs, sometimes even their legs. It was a way of showing that they were very manly and that they had the means of paying for them. It was a whim that was never cheap. Although later the public display of tattoos would end up being banned, it would again be tolerated. I saw it with my own eyes. And now even though tattoos have become the rage in so many parts of the world, in Japan, they still have a bad reputation because they're associated with the mafia.

Kimiko decided to buy a penthouse facing the castle because she wanted a beautiful view besides wanting to live in an old neighborhood. One of the most powerful *shoguns* in history, Tokugawa Ieyasu, had the castle constructed as a residence for his son, Yoshinao. He decided to build it in a spot where there was a small abandoned castle on flat ground with enough water and desirable vegetation. Since this was the mid-way point between Tokyo and Osaka, the castle would also serve as a bulwark in case there were attacks from the south. Tokugawa made sure to leave his family and the next generations power, land, and wealth. In order to avoid locating the fortress in the middle of nowhere, Ieyasu transplanted a complete town, with everything including its temples, around the castle. That was essentially the foundation of Nagoya, which, from that time onward, continued growing around the fortress.

The condominium was two streets from the Castle wall but from the ninth floor we could see the moat, two turrets and the whole castle with its two gigantic golden dolphins, one looking north and the other, south. The view was splendid because that beautiful structure was surrounded by trees, rivers, and canals. How I loved going out for walks early in the morning and seeing the willows whose shaggy branches seemed to dip into the water! And Toshi-chan used to sit on the wide balcony from seven to nine at night to contemplate all that. I often asked myself what he must be thinking about so deeply, although in my heart I never worried because I knew he was a very cultured, sane man without problems. His face said it all: he looked at the castle out of pleasure and nothing else.

It was lovely to live in the *shitamachi*, or old part of town. The houses and businesses that survived the war were witnesses of what the city became once upon a time. When the Tokugawa inhabited the Castle (various generations had lived there for 250 years), it was the commercial area of merchants and artisans. With the passage of time, it became a desirable neighborhood because the small old businesses were still there and because there was nostalgia for a preindustrial society. Because of that, there were still old workshops that specialized in dolls or ceramics, businesses where they sewed *futons*, fish-markets, and even a shop where tofu was made. That place held one of the city's few remaining *ichiba* or markets. It was small and had none of the variety and abundance of our markets in Mexico but there we could buy flowers, fruit, vegetables, meat, fish, *tsukemono* or pickled vegetables and ready-made *tempura*. How we enjoyed going to the market! Why was it that our traditions were so similar? Aside from the market, there were places like the one that specialized in *soba* or buckwheat noodles. Anybody might ask himself or herself who the customers in those places would be if none of the tourists visiting the Castle came to the neighborhood. As if they were guided to shop only along the main avenue leading to the wall. But it was magic, that Japanese magic that knows how to attract customers even to hidden places.

Without a doubt, I preferred living in *shitamachi*, near the castle, although it wasn't in the city-center. We had to take the metro in Sengencho and then transfer to go anywhere else. It wasn't easy but living in front of the castle had no price. On the other hand, when we lived in Sakae, next to the Central Park, we were in the very center of the city. The Nagoya metro wasn't like the one in Mexico City; it was older and noisy but it ran with a heavenly efficiency. As soon as you entered the station, you heard voices announcing the arrival or departure of a train. Besides, it ran precisely on the schedule inscribed in black letters and numbers on a white board. Tickets were bought in the machines and the charge was by distance traveled; everything was clearly specified on the route-map. When you entered the turnstile, the ticket was recorded and you kept it since you had to pass it through the exiting turnstile. None of this "I lost the ticket," because you'd have to pay what you owed right there. There was always an official in the ticket-booth in charge of those issues, among other things. Once you stepped onto the platform, wherever you directed your gaze would be covered by advertisements, even the seats of the benches. There were always at least two people in charge of controlling the flow of people. Japanese people are very respectful and would wait in line behind the security stripe but those in charge were always alert in case a lot of people arrived and they had to thin out the crowd or in case of an emergency. In cities like Tokyo or Osaka, those are the workers in charge of pushing passengers inside the subway car during rush-hour when the trains are full. That didn't happen in Nagoya because it wasn't such a populous city.

The interiors of the subway cars were and are very modern. The seats are made of velvet and there's air-conditioning. The insides are also crammed with announcements and from the ceiling also hang dozens of well-designed pages that advertise films, deodorants, magazines, exhibitions, vitamins, trips to Pacific islands, and so many other items that sometimes you don't have time to read them all. You hear a voice that never stops. It's the automatic voice that announces the station you're in as well as the next one; the final destination of the train; and all the businesses and services that can be found near the stations. Even though this is another kind of advertising, it's ideal because people are reminded where things are or are informed about them if they don't know. In general, there are two conductors, one in front, and the other in back. The two are duly dressed in uniforms consisting of blue trousers, white gloves, a navy-blue cap, a white shirt, and on the sleeve a badge that says "Transportation Bureau—City of Nagoya." They also wear a tag with their name in big letters. They are active conductors because they keep watch, opening and closing doors. Both communicate through gestures and whistles hanging around their necks.

What's fabulous is that there are talking vending-machines to buy tickets. Those are for blind or old people, or whomever has problems reading. Besides that, many stations are equipped with free bathrooms, seats, and rentable closets as well. Something that always seemed incredible to me was a blackboard located next to the ticket-booth, near the exit turnstiles. There was always a piece of chalk so that people could leave messages in case something was lost or for emergencies. The blackboard had lines on it and at the beginning of each there was a space for the hour and minutes. This forced the user to begin his or her message at the exact moment he or she began writing. It was fantastic because that way, people avoided getting lost or having to wait in vain for their friends or family members when there were rushes or changes in plans. At the end of the day, the blackboard was erased or if it got filled up in the course of the day, was erased little by little. No, the Nagoya metro isn't as beautiful as Mexico City's, with its murals, art, and exhibitions, but it's practical and efficient. Besides, it's a means of transportation used by poor and rich people, children and the elderly. In that space, there aren't differences or exclusions. In fact, it's assumed that taking the metro is an act that benefits society because it doesn't pollute the city so much. It isn't just for the masses, as it's thought to be in some countries.

It was very noisy when we lived near the Sakae station, or let's say, next to the Central Park. At night the *bosozoku* came out, reckless drivers who took out their cars to race them around the park. Their cars were low-slung, with thick tires, and they kept the windows open with music blaring. Their horns were scandalous and they laid on them as if they were deaf. To top it off, the troublemakers ran through traffic lights. Not even the police could handle them and even less so because there were so many of them: they came out by the dozen. At times there were more than a hundred. It was very strange because at that time, the Japanese police were supposed to be capable of capturing almost all offenders or criminals. Instead, the *bosozoku* almost seemed to mock them. With their bleached hair and hostile faces, they never got tired of going around and around the park. To cap it off, the city had been planned with broad avenues to ease auto traffic in various directions because the Toyota, Honda, and Mitsubishi plants were barely on its outskirts. For the *bosozoku* that was perfect because they felt like the masters of the city when it got dark. They raced everywhere, not only in the city-center. How they made others hate them! They also were members of the mafia or were connected with it in some way. People complained so much about the noise that without realizing it, they always carried them like a bad taste in the mouth. One day I heard about some macabre practices by the mafia. It was assumed that all of them were loyal to their bosses, loyal to the death. So, if someone committed an act against the boss or his group, there was the possibility that he'd have to go through a ritual called *yubitsume*.

Yubitsume is the act of cutting off part of the pinkie. This is done with a single slice of a razor or knife. Afterwards, the amputated part is wrapped in a cloth and solemnly presented to the boss. It's a way of showing remorse. If the mafia member keeps making mistakes, the amputation continues with other fingers. They say that there were gangs who'd been completely mutilated. Something almost unbelievable happened once. Inagawa Kakuji, one of the mafia bosses and thus head of one of the most powerful groups, wanted to put an end to the practice of *yubitsume*. He wanted above all to make a new rule so that members stopped cutting off their fingers. When it was learned that one of his own had asked a subordinate to cut off a finger, he called him in and severely reprimanded him. Feeling ashamed for being disrespectful to the boss, the accused man cut off his own finger and went to offer it to him as a sign of his repentance. *Tusukuribanashi mitai*. In effect, this seems like a made-up story but that's how life is, what can we do?

What I miss most about Nagoya is its *shitamachi*. That part of the city had seen everything, including the bombing that brought down the castle during WWII. Only the wall, three turrets and the second door in front survived. The rest was reconstructed. But even so, its striking elegance was a blessing to behold. The city suffered one of the worst attacks because it was the most important industrial center producing war materiel. In fact right there were built more than ten thousand bombers that the Japanese army fought with. But the *shitamachi* truly embodied a taste of the past, of tradition, of those beautiful, preindustrial times.

A view of the Nagoya Castle and the city from the Tezuka penthouse, 1984.

At the pool of the Nagoya Castle Hotel where Araceli saw the mafiosos
with enormous tattoos, 1984.

The wide streets of downtown Nagoya in 1981, perfect for the *bosozoku*
(reckless drivers).

Yakyū to Sumō
(Baseball and Sumō Wrestling)

To put it plainly, I didn't understand a thing about baseball. In Japan the only sports shown on TV were baseball and *sumō* wrestling. I remember in middle school, a friend, who wasn't at all a braggart, told me that he was a catcher. One day he invited all of us to go to one of his games so we went. I cheered when people cheered but that was all. I didn't understand it. Besides, the game seemed very slow and boring. When I returned home, my family asked me who'd won and I don't know if it was out of foolishness or distraction but I told them that I hadn't even found out. Oh, but if only it had been a soccer match because for that I was always in the first row of bleachers. Soccer excited me more than it did any of my girlfriends. How I missed watching soccer in Japan! At that time, soccer was almost unknown in that country. We're talking about twenty years before the World Cup in Korea-Japan. So it was difficult to convey to them the enthusiasm for and tradition of soccer in Mexico. How to tell them that Brazil had won the 1970 World Cup? How to explain to them that players like Pelé, Bobby Charlton, Beckenbauer, "El Nene," and Gianni Rivera had competed in Mexico's biggest stadiums? I felt that I had much to say but that they understood little. And, it may seem like a lie but little by little I had to become acquainted with baseball.

They explained it to me little by little: the position of the players, the pitcher, the catcher, the bases, the right-, second-, and third-basemen, the umpires and even the baseball diamond, the pitcher's mound, the foul-line, the foul-poles and everything else, I learned everything; badly, but I learned it. At that time, I was living in Nagoya and since destiny had brought me there, I had no other option than to cheer for the *Chūnichi Dragons* because if not, it would have been like being from Guadalajara and being a fan of *Pachuca*. As it turned out, people from Nagoya were so fanatic about *yakyū*, yes, about baseball, because this was one of the few foreign sports that had its own name in Japanese, that I too became a fan of the *Chūnichi Dragons*. I understood little about the matter of leagues and only knew that the *Dragons* were in the Central League, which also included their rivals, the *Yomiuri Giants* and the *Hanshin Tigers*, some of the teams that inspired fear. I was only happy seeing my new team win. The Japanese are serious about that. They do everything in a group. It was thrilling to see them win, even it was only on TV. And then the celebration, but a real celebration with *chuhai, sake* or beer, and of course with tons of food.

I ended up going to the stadium to see my team, of course. Japanese stadiums are rarely small and that was perfect because in Mexico I only knew the huge Azteca and Toluca stadiums when we went to see a Mexico vs. Canada match and the score ended up a tie. The Japanese fans seemed strange to me at first, since everything was so thoroughly organized. Instead of putting on the jerseys of the team, they often wore Japanese *hanten* or short waist-length robes and their *hachimaki* or headscarves. As always, Japanese people feel better in a group. In a group everything turns out better. So as far as cheering, it was fantastic because the whole stadium roared. They carried their big drums and long vertical banners. I don't know how to explain it but when you were among those fans, you felt strong and protected. What surprised me was that they took turns, even with cheering. In Mexican soccer that didn't happen, fans always cheered at the same time, none of this "we're going to wait until they're done before we begin." But in Japan, that wasn't the case, even in games there was respect because the fans waited until the other side's fans finished before they could begin.

I don't know when it happened but I became almost fanatic about baseball and I never managed to understand completely why. If I remember correctly, the *Chūnichi Dragons* earned the League Title in 1982. At that time, my favorite player was Hoshino Sen'ichi. Aside from being handsome, what a great player he was! He was a front-line pitcher who by the time the team won the Title, had already pitched for them for 14 years. The *Dragons* team was established in 1936 and had won the championship a few times. They still remembered that historical year of 1954 when they won the Central League title and their first Series in Japan. It was a glorious year because before that date they were called the *Nagoya Dragons* and long before that, they'd had other names, but in 1954 they prevailed and also got the sponsorship of the *Chūnichi Shimbun*, Nagoya's most important newspaper. Years later, I had a good laugh watching the film *Mr. Baseball*, in which Jack Elliot, a lousy American baseball player, decides to go to Japan to play with the *Chūnichi Dragons*. When he joins the team, he doesn't understand Japanese culture and, because of his lack of understanding, openly fights with Uchiyama, the manager. But putting that aside, the night that the *Dragons* won in 1982, I was at the home of some friends. There were about ten of us. It occurred to us to get on our motorbikes and go to a *robatayaki* to eat and continue celebrating. We felt like the rulers of the universe. We raced at a hundred miles per hour and nothing could touch us. Nobody cared about speeding that night. The important thing was that our team had won. Yes, our excitement and drinking went on and on. Since there were TVs everywhere, in bars and restaurants, and even outside some buildings, we boasted to each other as we watched, over and over, the replay of that epic finale of the game. And that wasn't all. The following day the shops and department stores had already hung immense, beautiful signs that said something like "Congratulations *Chūnichi*! In honor of our team, today everything is reduced 25%." Yes, they celebrated in style. Well, there was so much enthusiasm that the restaurants and bars took casks of *sake* out to the street and offered food and drink to whomever passed by. In Nagoya I joined them as if I'd been born right there and leapt and shouted with them: "*Banzai, banzai, banzai, banzai!*" Of course, absolutely!

Since the time I was a girl, I'd passionately followed sports. The few Olympics I'd seen I watched from beginning to end. At home I had a desk-drawer filled with newspaper clippings of articles about and photos of Nadia Comaneci. And, one day when I watched a program about Jesse Owens, my heart almost melted when I saw what had happened in the 1936 Berlin Olympics. So I began to collect his photos little by little. As a girl, I felt entranced seeing my team, the *Águilas del América*. Please don't tell me that I'm a peasant. In the neighborhood where I grew up, you either cheered for the *América* or *Las Chivas*, period and end of story. That was it. What did you expect me to do? Cheer for those wacky *Chivas*? If because of that, I'd already been born with many faults, I didn't need any others. My family was finally sold on the idea; first they were fans of the *América* and then when that little-known team began to gain fame and fortune, they changed teams, just like that, as if it were as easy as changing clothes. Now they're fans of *Cruz Azul*. I'm telling you that sooner or later, people reveal their own faults.

In Nagoya every once in a while, I ended up feeling very close to Mexico. One night:

"Hello."

"Hello. Uhhh, good evening."

"How may I help you?"

"May I speak with Pipino Cuevas?"

"He's not here. Who's calling?"

"This is . . . Araceli. . . one of his fans. . . ."

"I'm sorry but the gentleman can't be disturbed. . . ."

"Whom do I have the pleasure of speaking to?"

"His manager."

"But I'm one of the few Mexican women living in Nagoya and . . ."

"I understand but boxers can't speak with anyone the night before a fight."

"I understand too, but . . ."

"Who told you where we were staying?"

"My contacts. Right here, in Nagoya."

"I'm very sorry, Miss."

"Me, too, but ok . . . anyway, tomorrow we're going to win."

"I hope so."

"Good night and till tomorrow at the arena."

"Thanks. Till tomorrow."

That was the first time that I went to see a boxing match. I'd seen *Rocky* and *Rocky II* I don't know how many times. At home my family were fans of the legendary Cassius Clay and also of the Mexican boxers of 1968. They chatted nostalgically about Ricardo Delgado and Antonio Roldán, both gold-medal winners; one in the flyweight and the other in the feather-weight category. They also spoke about Joaquín Rocha and Agustín Zaragoza, bronze-medal winners. International boxing matches almost never came to Nagoya, so for that reason it was a great occasion, above all because a Mexican boxer would be fighting. The sprinkling of sweat and blood I'd seen so much on TV didn't disgust me, so I waited for that day with pleasure.

The afternoon of the fight was cool and clear. Kimiko begged me to put on a red *mariachi sombrero* with silver filigree. I didn't want to look so folkloric but I agreed because I didn't want to regret it afterwards if I hadn't worn it. Compared to making myself ridiculous the night before by calling up the boxer, wearing a *sombrero* would be nothing. We took the subway to Meijō Kōen and walked to the arena through the park. As we got closer, I realized that everyone was walking hurriedly, as if they'd lost something. There wasn't a single foreign or Mexican face, just waves and waves of Japanese ones. We didn't know what seats we had because we'd bought the tickets on short notice. The arena was full but to our luck, we were in the second tier and everything looked very close. First they played the Mexican national anthem and then the Japanese one. And the fight began. From the first round I was biting my nails. I was sweating bricks, as if I'd been a regular fan of boxing. Mexican boxers were nothing new in Japan. Since 1960, dozens of them had made appearances to challenge world titles in the lightweight, feather-weight, flyweight, welter-weight, and bantam-weight categories. In effect, Rubén Olivares had fought in 1971 and surprised the public so much that people said his fight made history. As with everything, the Japanese took boxing very seriously. They even have a day to celebrate it: May 19 is "Boxing Day" in that country.

It wasn't the first time that Pipino Cuevas had stepped on Japanese soil. Being already the welter-weight champion, in 1976 he traveled to Japan, where he'd made an amazing debut. The interesting thing is that he became a professional boxer at the age of fourteen. The day of the fight, as I was watching him, it was obvious that he hit with brute strength besides being in excellent physical condition. He moved in the ring with such speed that you barely saw his foot-work. And at the moment of throwing his punches, he did so with such strength that you never saw where his gloves were coming from. I can't seem to recall the name of his adversary but it was a very close fight. The rounds became longer. At every moment it seemed as if Pipino was going to lose and then, *zas zas zas*, a cross, a hook, and an *upper-cut* left the Japanese boxer tottering. We heard the referee: *"Time! Stop!"* And the audience with clenched fists and worried faces begging God to sound the bell. Then the twelfth round and the boxers were so worn out that I thought they were going to stop the fight and decide the winner by points. But to my great surprise, in the thirteenth round, Pipino gave his opponent such a knockout punch that it left him bouncing off the ropes until he couldn't stand anymore and fell to the floor right there. "Bravo! Bravo! Bravo!" I began to shout as I leapt up. How strange to be among thousands of people and to come out winning. We wanted to get close to the ring, but it was impossible. If I'd been able to have done it, I would have offered my *sombrero* to him like fans do with Mexicans abroad. The Japanese are always so pleasant, they offered me congratulations although it may have been with resigned faces. Kimiko was delighted. My innocence prevented me from realizing that she was happy when she saw me content. We left drunk with joy and walked slowly through the park beneath the light of a half-moon.

But more than boxing, there's a weird sport that makes the Japanese crazy. I sounded like a broken record every time they asked me:

"Where are you from?"

"Mexico."

"Oh, really?"

"Yes, that's right."

"—Mekishiko, mmm, that's where the "Santo," "Blue Damon" and the "Mil Máscaras" are from."

"Exactly, that's where they're from."

I don't know how many times I ended up having the same conversation. It seemed strange that they knew so much about wrestling in Mexico. The good thing is that one of my obsessions had been watching the films of Santo el Enmascarado de Plata. So when they asked, it excited me to talk about one of my childhood idols, of course! I told them that I knew about wrestling above all through the films where El Santo confronted monsters, murderers, mummies, vampire-women, crazy doctors, mafiosos, and all those who wanted to do evil. Above all I remembered Santo Against the Vampire-Women and while my Japanese barely allowed it, I explained to them, although with gestures, that El Santo had to fight with vampire-women in that forgotten castle full of dusty catacombs, but thanks to convertible cars and clocks, the Enmascarado de Plata could leave with what belonged to him. I also told them about the film The Treasure of Moctezuma because I loved the suspense when that dangerous gang wanted to rob the treasure of the Aztec Emperor. And don't even mention The Mummies of Guanajuato, which surely was a film that scared me but one I also liked. Their jaws dropped when I began to explain to them what mummies are because it was something that people there hadn't heard about. It was as if I were a wind-up doll and I couldn't stop so I kept talking about Santo Against Doctor Death and all the women he went out with and how they were almost always at the point of taking off his mask. The Santo was still alive at that time so people spoke about him in the present tense. He still possessed the magic and mystery of a great wrestler, a true hero who makes a deep impression on a child, an adolescent, or anyone who likes clean, pure sport disguised as drama, all those capable of seeing the ring turned into theater.

Since I was so involved with wrestling, they asked me if I liked sumō. I was never good at lying and I had a hard time saying that I didn't understand it and that honestly it didn't amuse me. At that time I'd learned that being honest and answering "No" ended up sounding very bad in Japanese. You had to say something like "Well, the truth is that *sumō* seems like a very interesting sport and little by little I'm learning its rules." Japanese is a very smooth language that doesn't allow harshness. But language aside, just as I'd entered the world of baseball, little by little and with blind faith, I began to love *sumō*.

Summers in Nagoya were hell on earth. The humidity not only made us sweat rivers all day, before and after bathing, but it even left us lightheaded. You couldn't think about anything, good or bad. You went out to the street, you walked half a block and you were already soaked in sweat again. *Mushiatsui* is the name given to this oppressive and unbearable heat. At least there was a name for that purgatory you had to suffer for months. The humidity created a mist that made your eyes tear. You could barely distinguish anything. Then from a distance, you could make out the young *sumō* wrestlers walking by in their *yukata*, a cotton Japanese robe worn in summer, and their sandals, or *getas*. When I saw them, I realized that those wrestlers had come to the city for the Nagoya Tournament, which lasted two weeks. What luck to be able to see that legendary Japanese sport —in existence for more than 2,000 years— right there, because the championships only take place in Tokyo, Osaka, Fukuoka, and Nagoya. When I still didn't get it, I couldn't fathom how anyone could be interested in a fight that lasts only seconds. Someone who doesn't understand *sumō* is first impressed by the corpulence of the wrestlers and their costume, which is only a loincloth. Being a wrestler isn't an easy thing because he must measure more than five feet, five inches in height and weigh at least 176 pounds. When a young man has those attributes and shows interest, he goes to live in a communal house, a kind of compound, like for priests, and there he and others follow a strict life with rules, hierarchies, order, respect, training, a special diet, and a number of other things. The wrestlers who are married go to the compound in the morning and take their leave at night, to sleep in their respective houses.

As with everything, at first, the youngest ones have to clean the compound, prepare the meals, wash the dishes, and help in any way they can. To the envy of many women, who supposedly spend their lives on a diet to slim down, wrestlers do the opposite. Their "diet" consists precisely of eating well in order to gain weight and keep healthy at the same time. They eat various types of mega-soups called *chanko-nabe* that contain vegetables, rice or noodles, beef, chicken, fish, and various condiments. Although the wrestlers don't look at all agile, the truth is that their bodies are as strong as those of weight-lifters. They get up very early to exercise for a few good hours, then they eat, sleep a while in the afternoon and later on do lighter exercise. But their training doesn't end there because they also study anatomy, physical education, the history of *sumō*, calligraphy and *jinku*, a kind of ancient singing.

Frankly, I had no head for philosophizing about a sport that was the opposite of baseball. One of them ended in seconds and the other lasted hours. One was a rapid fight in which what mattered was strength and swift defeat; the other was democratic because the two teams had the same opportunity to pitch and go to bat. One was a genuine Japanese sport that had existed since ancient times when wrestlers fought before the Emperor, then became a martial art employed by warriors but in reality was practiced as a vocation by real athletes who were disposed to sacrifice whatever was necessary; the other was a sport imported from the West that was barely a few decades old. But both sports were a synthesis of what Japan embodied because while the Japanese were very much in their element with their ancient wrestlers, they were also very Western because they always wanted to do what the Europeans or Americans did. It was for that reason that they were so fanatic about baseball and such fervent admirers of golf and tennis, and at the same time there were many people, generally older, who were *aficionados* of *sumō*.

As if by a stroke of magic, I began to enjoy *sumō* with all its costumes, ceremonies, rituals, and drums. In fact, in *sumō*, the rituals are as important as the fight itself; maybe for that reason, the rituals are much longer than the fight. To begin with, the referee is dressed in the style of ancient warrior-hunters, in a kind of silk kimono embroidered with splendid golden thread. The rules of the game are very simple: the wrestler has to get his opponent out of the ring, or *dohyō*, to win. And on the other hand, the first wrestler who touches the floor or loses his loincloth or executes a forbidden move is eliminated. But before the fight, the *yokozuna*, or most advanced wrestlers, carry out what's known as the *yokozuna dohyō-iri*, which are harmonious movements in which each wrestler displays his powerful muscles at the same time that he scares away evil spirits. That ritual is carried out in the center of the ring, under the gaze of the referee and the other wrestlers.This kind of dance is complemented by the beauty of each wrestler's costume, the *keshōma-washi*, a colorful ceremonial apron of exquisite silk, embroidered in fine calligraphy, with symbols, animals, and the names of patrons. Witnessing that handsome spectacle was a true delight to behold. It got me wondering about how the Mayan ritual and ball game might have been, with its elaborate dress, its masks, its sounds, its music and all the extravagance of pre-Hispanic culture. But there I was, supporting those wrestlers whose magic attracted me like a magnet. I saw them as gods capable of holding up the earth and vanquishing the universe. I had the great fortune of living in Japan when great wrestlers were competing: Kitanoumi, Takanosato, Wakashimazu, and, for me, the greatest of all time, Chiyo no Fuji.

Born in Hokkaido, in the north of Japan, Chiyo no Fuji stood out by being much more slender than his opponents, although he had the same or greater strength than they did. He possessed all that a great wrestler needed: talent, strength, charisma, grace. He immediately became my idol and so, alone, unaccompanied, I went to see the tournament a couple of times. It was curious that near the ring, instead of seats, there were *tatami* or mats, like thick *petates*, and people were seated Japanese style, as if at a picnic. They sat there leisurely and on their mats they had food, *sake*, and beer. Everything was bought at the arena itself and so they enjoyed the various fights that took place throughout the day. The ring was a relatively small circle, without ropes, and was bordered by a line of rice on a kind of square clay platform about a half-yard high. In the northeast corner of the square there was bucket with salt and in the northwest corner there was another with *chikaramizu* water (power — if not to say holy— water) and a tray where they could spit. Over the ring was a hanging structure in the shape of an eaved roof, like the roof of a Shinto temple. From this structure hung four gigantic cords: green, white, red, and black. Each represented a season of the year.

Sumō is a typically Japanese sport but it's very similar to boxing and to wrestling. Today, there aren't many *sumō* wrestlers and there are only a few categories of competition. All the professional wrestlers, and the highest ranked ones, face each other and the one who wins the most fights wins the championship. The winner receives the Emperor's Cup, which in fact is much larger in size than the World Cup. But what I liked most about *sumō* was the respect shown between the two wrestlers. Before the fight, they first greeted each other with bows in the center of the ring. Next, they withdrew to their corners, doing exercises with their feet the way boxers do with their hands. Then the fighters crouched, in the center of the ring, each behind his line, and displaying all their strength, raised their hands and applauded. That was like a promise given to one's adversary that he would undertake the competition with clean hands. After that, each one turned toward his corner, rinsed his mouth with the *chikaramizu* and spit into the tray. Next, believe it or not, they grabbed fistfuls of coarse salt and scattered it on the floor. As all this was happening, the wrestlers studied, intimidated, and observed each other with looks that could kill; then, eventually they went back to their own spots, ready to begin the fight. It's a physical as well as psychological contest because the wrestlers, by pure intuition, have to touch the floor at the same time in order to begin the fight.

How I enjoyed watching those rituals that were so elegant, those exquisite clothes, that fleeting confrontation that was like an erotic battle, where the lovers embrace and struggle not to surrender to each other. They fight for a moment that isn't measured by any clock but by a mysterious force where neither numbers, seconds, days on the calendar, nights, suns, nor anything else exists. The fight lasts an instant, like when one of two lovers can't stand it any longer and surrenders. For the spectator, that tiny moment is a lightning flash of joy, a climax that is lived intensely. In Japan I learned that life is full of small moments like that; and for that reason you have to enjoy them completely. In that spirit, I watched Chiyo no Fuji wrestle. For me, he was a god of flesh and blood. The only time that I saw him, I went up to him before and after the fight. Before the fight, he was wearing an elegant blue and white *yukata*. And afterwards, he'd put on a royal-blue towel, the same shade as his loincloth. I approached him and took a quick photo. Then, I touched his right shoulder. I felt like I'd touched Jesus Christ.

The arena where *sumō* took place was nothing like the arenas used for boxing or wrestling. People didn't leap or jump up, or cheer. They only applauded and enjoyed all the color, sound, ritual, and spectacle of it. I enjoyed everything, up to the last moment. Years later, I returned to Japan to see the 2002 World Cup. It was strange to watch soccer being played in Japan because in the eighties, that was something I'd neither experienced nor dreamed of seeing. Besides, now Nagoya is the proud owner of a professional soccer team, the *Nagoya Grampus Eight,* which is part of the *J-League.* And to top it off, they play in the Toyota Stadium, built for that 2002 World Cup. In the box where I now keep the few yellowed photos I still have from that time, I have five of the day when I saw Chiyo no Fuji fight. I took one from the front and another from the back and three of the ring. In that same box, I have a baseball signed by Hoshino. And, not long ago, when I was looking for who knows what on the Internet, I stumbled upon a video that shows the moment when *Santo el En-mascarado de Plata* took off his mask before Jacobo Zabludovski. I'd never watched that program. Cursed be the day I saw it. The *Santo* should have remained in my heart as that mysterious hero I never really saw or touched.

At the Nagoya Stadium watching the Chūnichi Dragons, 1982.

Chiyo no Fuji at Nagoya Basho, 1982.

Chiyo no Fuji in action at Nagoya Basho, 1982.

Pipino Cuevas at the boxing arena in Meijō Kōen, Nagoya,
1982.

Nihongo
(Japanese)

There's no doubt that speaking Japanese was all Greek to me. Well, speaking it isn't so difficult but writing it was another story. I arrived in Japan not knowing the language. All I had with me was a book that they used in the Japanese institute on Mártires Irlandeses Street, in Mexico City. A friend put it in my hands. The text was very clear and I began to figure it out by reading the vocabulary and the dialogues. It was written in what they call *kunreishikiromaji* or the transliteration of Japanese words to the Roman alphabet. The pronunciation is very simple and there are even words that sound like ours. For example, *kama* means pot, *ama* means a female pearl-diver, *kasa* is umbrella and *baka* means dumb. At first it made me laugh because I thought of an umbrella as if it were really a "casa" [or house] and of a dumb "vaca" [or cow] resting on the grass. The Japanese got their pictographic and ideographic characters from the Chinese. In fact, the only writing that's genuinely Japanese is based on phonetic symbols called *hiragana* and *katakana*; those are easy and are few in number compared to the Chinese characters that take forever to learn.

In order to learn to read, you have to write until you're exhausted. Students reach the first year of high school and still continue learning how to write. They dream about and sweat over their language; it traps them in their worst nightmares; they get on the subway and are analyzing words in the ads, counting their strokes, it never leaves them in peace. Because of their high educational level, there are books and magazines in every color and flavor. The whole country is like an infinite, almost overflowing, library. In the bookstores the comics and magazine sections were always packed with young people and adults addicted to reading. It didn't bother them to remain standing for up to two hours in order to devour those pages. If it had been up to them, they might have stayed longer but the lack of time or the pressure they felt when they didn't buy the book they were reading forced them to stop.

Kissaten means tea-house although at that time almost all of those establishments had been converted into cafeterias. After the war, these grew by leaps and bounds and suddenly began to sell coffee imported from Colombia, Brazil, and even Kilimanjaro. Since coffee, in some way, was always a luxury item, the cafeterias were elegantly decorated. In fact, when you entered them, you felt as if you were in a quiet, peaceful world. I'd been warned that the coffee was expensive but I didn't believe it until I checked it out myself. In Mexico, I'd gotten used to VIPS and to Toks, where they served us two or three cups of coffee for the same price. In Japan my first shock was that the cups looked lovely but were very small and, to top it off, they only served three-quarters of a cup because that was considered fancy. If you asked for a second cup, you had to pay for it. Since that time, I've learned to drink coffee slowly. Because of that, up till now I take a half-hour or more to finish one cup. When I was given lessons in the tea ceremony, I learned that you had to sip it as if it were the first and last time in your life you would enjoy it. I associated that with their way of drinking coffee; it was necessary to savor it little by little.

The cafeterias offered fabulous service and, especially in the summer, it was a refuge where I could sit comfortably in good air-conditioning. At first, I was given a little cold towel because it was summer but if it had been winter they would have given me a hot one. They prepared the coffee the old-fashioned way with a filter or strainer and served it along with some peanuts or sweets. They had a spacious area with newspapers, magazines, and comics, or *manga*. Because of that, many of the customers went there especially to read. I always leafed through fashion magazines and passionately enjoyed what was a new discovery for me: iced coffee; in Mexico I'd never drunk it. The décor always seemed refined and the background music was almost always classical. It was expensive sitting there to drink a cup of coffee but that atmosphere of quietude truly had no price.

It was in a cafeteria where I became a fan of the magazine *An-An*. The images in it spoke for themselves. It also seemed curious to me that magazines of this kind could be leafed through like ours. In other words, the cover and the page-order were like those we were used to, even though proper Japanese books were read from back to front. There were so many publications that twenty thousand magazines and close to twenty-five thousand books were published in just one year. Toshi-chan wasn't obsessed with reading although he religiously bought *Chūo Koron, Sekai* and *Pūrezidento.* They were very serious magazines that covered economics, history, and controversial issues. Common everywhere were the blessed *manga* for adults, young people, and children. Tons of those were sold. Their themes were so varied that people could choose between stories about samurais, cowboys, mafiosos, impossible loves, science fiction, prostitutes, outlaws, and demons. But that's not all; some of them were serious and explored themes relating to physics, math, or medicine. In this format there were also short novellas about fifty pages long. People drank them up because they were all illustrated.

When I was a girl, in my house we were always forbidden to read comic-books and those stories that were sold at the news-stands. Because of that, the *manga* was a new world for me, a dare as well. At least that's how it felt to me. In reality, they were easier to understand because of the illustrations. They were written in ideograms and also in *hiragana* so that children and young people could read them more easily. I remember that when I began to buy *manga,* one day, I had the embarrassment of my life. I got on the subway and started reading casually. After a good while, I looked up and a pair of high-school boys neatly dressed in uniforms were staring at me, dumbfounded. I didn't pay any attention to them and continued reading. Suddenly I managed to hear them whispering and innocently giggling:

"Did you see how long it takes her to read one page?"

"Yeah, about five hours. . . ."

I didn't lift my head. They obviously didn't realize that I wasn't Japanese. Those reactions never hurt my feelings because when the opposite happened and people found out that I was a foreigner trying to learn their language, they respected me with great fanfare.

"With the skills you have, you don't need to attend a Japanese-language school," remarked Adrian, an Australian who was taking classes with me. The truth is that everything happens backwards to me. First I learned the spoken language and then I went on to formally study it. I'd already learned *hiragana* and *katakana* on my own. Also, I'd already begun to learn *kanji* or the ideograms. It fascinated me so much that I began to fill complete notebooks. I used to repeat the same symbol thirty, fifty, a hundred or however many times until my inexperienced hand became familiar with it. I couldn't believe that the simplest characters were incredibly important words. With just four lines, I could create the word *kokoro;* it was like writing two pairs of accents and you were done. On the other hand, if you start to think about it, in our language it's much more complicated because we have to write seven letters and an accent: CORAZÓN [heart]. Other words made up of four strokes were *day, inside, father, moon, tree, water, fire, dog, weapon, sentence.* . . . However, in order to depict the symbols we barely used in writing, like *mouse, flute, turtle* or *dragon,* we had to learn their thirteen to fifteen strokes.

In the city where I lived, Japanese was taught at a couple of universities. The admission process and the tuition for the semester were prohibitive, unless you had a grant or were rich. In Tokyo, Kobe, or Osaka, it was another story. There was an absolute abundance of schools for foreigners in those cities. However, in Nagoya, aside from the university, classes were given at the YMCA and that was where I had my first formal lessons. I had fun with the Australians, Chinese, Americans, and Nepalese students. The last group had an incredible facility for language but they couldn't get the accent. They used to pronounce words like the Chinese do; they couldn't manage the "r"'s and they spoke too fast. However, when you're a Spanish speaker, pronunciation is both a fact and a gift. The only sound that's difficult for us is the "z," which is pronounced "ZZZZ," like the buzzing of a fly, and that's it.

My first classes were delightful because I began to learn the structure of the language. Before, I'd learned by mechanical repetition, the use of a dictionary, and intuition. I'd never questioned anything, not even why the verb comes at the end of the sentence. It was like saying: *Tomorrow school going I'm thinking of,* instead of *I'm thinking of going to school tomorrow.* I also never asked myself about the most obvious thing, which was the lack of articles or the use of the plural form. For example, *hito* means *person* and *hitotachi, persons* or *people.* I'll never forget when I began to add the ending *tachi* to everything that I wanted to change to plural; and once I cried out: *kireiyamatachi.* What I meant to say was *kirei na yama* or *pretty mountain* or *pretty mountains.* In reality the plural doesn't exist as we conceive of it. Those who heard me express myself burst into fits of laughter. *Kawaii. . . ! How adorable!* I must have seemed like a child making innocent but unforgiveable mistakes. Even years later, they reminded me: "Do you remember your *yamatachi*?" We always recalled my expression with laughter and nostalgia.

The word *kami* means *god* and also *paper.* They're homophones. Japanese is full of such terms. Although of course, when *kami* is written with Chinese characters, they are two completely different symbols because *god* is written with three lines and *paper* with ten. I always thought, laughing in between, that the Japanese had a relationship with paper as if it were in reality a god. They spend so many years learning their language that they live with paper in their hands. And that is the only way of learning how to write, through repetition. As for myself, a blister kept popping out on my middle finger from writing the same symbol so many times. The only good thing was that I'd always liked copying texts and more texts in my notebooks, like the ancient scribes. In summer I would fill entire notebooks in pencil. It felt like a good exercise to improve my handwriting. The Japanese always admired the fact that I dedicated myself with such gusto to their language. The Chinese were also highly disciplined, except that they beat me at that battle because they already had the advantage of knowing the symbols and I didn't. But if writing in that country was an art, paper was too. It was common to spend up to an hour deciding what type of paper to buy to write letters or also when you chose notebooks for school. And when I bought envelopes, I frankly became dizzy. Envelopes were used to give monetary gifts for weddings, graduations, bonuses, and even funerals. So I spent hours contemplating the designs in paper made from rice, straw, and cotton.

With my notebook in hand, I used to go to practice at a cafeteria that I liked because its atmosphere couldn't be more Japanese. It was close to Sengencho, where we lived. Time had stopped there and the truth is that it wasn't as sophisticated as all the other cafeterias except that it still bore traces of the old tea-houses. It had old tables and chairs; the coffee-cups were old, too. It was like stepping into one of those old cafés in the center of Mexico City. The owner was a little old lady who ran the business not because she needed the money but to keep herself busy. She always wore an impeccable *kimono* and a starched white apron with sleeves, typical for Japan. It opened at 4:00 in the morning and was frequented by a world of people who came from who-knows-where. It offered a *"morning set"* or complete breakfast until 10:00 in the morning, which consisted of coffee, a piece of fruit, toast, and sliced cabbage beneath a fried egg with ketchup. That was their idea of a complete American breakfast. I went there because I could speak with everyone and because it had a huge library with *manga*, and books on architecture, gardening, art, and fashion. Besides that, it had collections of film posters, Japanese antiques, *origami* globes that hung from the ceiling, ceramic *maneki neko*, statues of Buddha, and lanterns. Although the place was crowded with objects, something uncommon in Japan, it fascinated me. I felt happy in that environment, which was so Japanese and so sincere, without pretensions. I used to sit there for hours and fill entire notebooks, trying to memorize sentences and symbols.

I finally left Japan for good speaking a lot and writing little, although I suppose that that's the feeling of almost all foreigners. But I took refuge in studying its language and continued studying it from a distance, with a real desire to learn. I didn't want to let it go because I felt as if someone were ripping away something that was very much mine. I wanted it to stay with me for a long time, forever. Thanks to that, I was lucky enough to read *Sarada kinenbi* (*Salad Anniversary*), the immortal book of the then-young poet Tawara Machi, two years after its publication, at the end of the eighties. It was as if Sor Juana Inés de la Cruz had been reincarnated in the twentieth century. What she did was to take the *tanka*, a very traditional short form of poetry, to speak about daily modern life. This hadn't occurred to anyone. In her poems she speaks about love, disillusion, travels, food, and mundane subjects. What's so beautiful about them is that she expresses this using a classical form as a point of departure. She says in one of her poems:

> *Sayonara ni mukatte*
> *Asa ga kuru koto no*
> *namida no aji de*
> *omereto o yaku*

> The goodbye draws near
> morning arrives
> this omelette I fry
> tastes of tears

> *Nandemonai kaiwa*
> *nandemonai waragao*
> *nandemonai kara*
> *furusato ga suki*

> Conversation without meaning
> sunny face without sense
> because it's meaningless
> I adore my home town

> *'Yomesan ni*
> *nareyo' da nante*
> *kanchuhai nihon de itte*
> *shimatte ii no.*

"Marry me"
after two drinks
what exactly
are you trying to say?

Another book I couldn't have enjoyed more was Mishima's *Shiosai*. It's a love story between Shinji and Hatsue, two young people who live in a small fishing village. If Tawara's book is poetically beautiful, Mishima's prose is glorious. *Shiosai* is written in a language that's delicate, perfect, exquisite. What a beautiful story! And an essay that fascinated me was *In ei raisan*, by Tanizaki Jun'ichiro. The way he describes the soul of the Japanese aesthetic through examples of light and shadows is incomparable.

I hurt down to my bones from the experience of reading in Japanese. It was a desperate situation having to consult the dictionary so many times to get past one page. And it wasn't just about looking for words in alphabetical order like we do with our dictionaries but that you often have to count the number of lines in each symbol to identify it by its strokes. It requires a patience that has to be cultivated with time. It's like learning to meditate or pray. I remember that I would often use the expression *isshōkenmei ganbarimasu*, "I will do my best." When I stumbled upon the characters that describe that expression, I became paralyzed. It's written with more than thirty strokes and literally says: "to guard a place with one's life." In other words, in the past it meant "putting one's life on the line" but today it means to do something with everything you've got, till you die. My classmates used to laugh when they saw me practice writing that symbol, which was so complicated. "You do everything *the best you can*," they told me, "Aren't you watching me?" I answered.

I never felt guilty about having learned *nihongo*, that is, formal Japanese, until later. *Rokujyu no tenarai*, as they say, which means, "it's never too late to start."

Mekishiko to Nihon
(Mexico and Japan)

Not long ago, I read Juan Villoro's article "The Sands of Japan." It's truly marvelous. What would we do in Mexico if we didn't have writers like him? Only Mexican writers can describe Japanese things with a Mexican flair; and it's a fact that they don't need to embellish them. If they tried to do so, it would be enough for them to describe the landscape of our land, the *fiestas*, the food; nothing else would be necessary. What's ours was born like that, embellished. And what's Japanese doesn't need flourishes because it's naturally delicate and exquisite. What luck Villoro had going to Japan in the year 2009. One hundred years earlier, the poet Efrén Rebolledo was also there. But he ran into bad luck because the war caught up with him. No, that war didn't reach Japan but was fought right here, in our own land when the Mexican Revolution erupted. Since Rebolledo had been sent by the country's most important leaders, when we Mexicans began to fight one against the other, he remained over there not lacking a master but a boss. And the poor man had to return. They say that he went begging for money in order to buy his return ticket. What rotten luck. But even with that he wrote books about Japan during the time he was there.

Destiny arrives when she feels like it. I went to stay in Japan because my friends Yano Kunihiko and Yoshimoto Tatsu were from there and I suddenly had the urge to go to their country; although I also confess that as a girl I was a fan of *Señorita Cometa* and *Los Agentes Fantasmas* [The Ghost Agents]. I worked in an office from 1980 to 1981 and from that I saved money for my ticket. At that time money still had value. Now it no longer does. Once there,

I went wild over the place and stayed a year-and-a-half. When I returned to Mexico, I missed Japan so much that I decided to return once more for a year. All that happened between 1981 and 1984. When I lived there I was so inexperienced about everything that all I could do was write letters and whole pages of *kanji*. I didn't write anything else. To top it off, my sister, the one who was taking care of my mother in her old age, stupidly threw all those letters away. All that's left are my own memories. If I'd gotten there with experience or had been born with the gift of writing, I would have written these pages right there but it wasn't like that. In spite of everything, I don't blame myself because to paraphrase Guillermo Sheridan, a highly cultured critic who has deeply studied Mexicans interested in Japan, it also went very badly for Octavio Paz in Japan. He says that Paz wandered around there about 1952. At that time, one didn't find riches but a lot of misery. Japan had just lost the war and had barely cleared away the rubble. Paz didn't like that country at all and said, better to escape something than to die right there. . . . Sheridan says that because of that he ended up writing this heart-rending poem:

"There's No Escape?"

Everything's far away, there's no return, the dead aren't dead, the living no longer living,
there's a wall, an eye that's a pit, everything is tossed there, the body, thoughts weigh down, all time is
right this minute collapsing endlessly. . . . [5]

But even with all that, afterward he set himself to the task of writing very beautiful poems, Japanese-style. He also made the book *Sendas de Oku* [The Narrow Road to Oku] understandable. Thanks to him, we can comprehend it. So, even if things went badly for him there, at least he dedicated himself to teaching us something about that country.

The Mexican who truly understood Japan was José Juan Tablada. There are those who keep saying that Tablada never went to Japan. That's what Jorge Ruedas de la Serna said, and I believe it because he's a very wise gentleman, a professor through and

---

[5] Quoted by Guillermo Sheridan in *Poeta con paisaje. Ensayos sobre la vida de Octavio Paz*. Mexico: Era, 2004, p. 456.

through. It turns out that Tablada invented *En el país del sol.* And in the end, did that kill anyone? What must be respected is that Don Tablada understood the soul of Japanese poetry more than any other Mexican did. In Japanese the word for *soul* is *tamashī* but it's not used like that. Soul would better be expressed as *kokoro.* I believe that he understood that best because his *haiku* are the best that have been written in Spanish. And if anyone doesn't like that, well, I pity them. But never mind. Only he understood how to describe insects, animals and Mexican landscapes, revealing their souls to all of us. But to show their essence, it wasn't necessary to make them Japanese because they'd been born in our land and what's from here is from here. What he did instead was to borrow a little of Japan's sun. With that opening he illuminated Mexican things; because of that they began to breathe with a Japanese air. The sun in Mexico shines more than in Japan although it's hotter over there. The *saboten,* as the Japanese call the *nopal* cactus, is from our land and only grows to its full height here, completely free. Because of that its blooms have the most unique color in the world. Tablada understood all this. At bottom what he wanted was for us to understand that there's another way of looking at our plants and our landscape and because of that, in whatever way he could, he made them Japanese. In order to write well about Japan, you must understand not light but shadow. If Tablada and Tanizaki Jun'ichiro had met, they would have understood each other very well. They would have been able to speak at great length about how in Japan shade is disappearing more all the time and how in Mexico the sun is also vanishing. This happens when people stop sowing their own land and begin to import foreign things and adopt foreign customs.

Our poet truly understood art. He loved the painter Hiroshigue; he saw him as a god capable of painting his land the way it presented itself. Because of that he respected him so much and on afternoons became lost admiring his paintings. And, like the Japanese, Tablada also illustrated one of his books and wrote his poetry in the form that the Mexican painters paint our landscape, using bold and wise colors, colors that only a Mexican hand could paint. Always generous, thanks to him, Miguel "El Chamaco" Covarrubias opened up a path for himself in New York and later painted his murals of the Pacific. If Tablada introduced *haiku* to the Spanish language, before him, the wise Alfonso, no, not Alfonso the Wise, but Reyes, had already written at least one haiku:

"Hai-kai de Euclides"

Parallel lines
converge
only when they reach infinity.

And there have been so many Mexicans who have written
haiku that it would take a lifetime to study and name them although
I admit that I like this one written by the poet Manuel Maples Arce:

With a single dripping note
the water insisted
without arguments.

Oh, that people from that land of noisy birds. From there have
emerged so many musicians, muralists and poets. In Mexico the *haiku*
is respected so much that even children from almost forgotten towns
in Campeche write them.

And it's a fact that there are now good Mexican poets living
in Japan as is the case of Aurelio Asiain, who writes:

"Rotenburo" [Outdoor Bath]

A few words
in the green evaporated
shade,
cypresses caressing
the water's edge.

"Rekindling"
For Adolfo Castañon

A silver bridge.
And even if gold, it would be enough
for a big house
in the suburbs.
Now it's peopled by ghosts.

His work is important because aside from writing poetry, he
translates Japanese poets so that they're available for Mexicans and
for those who read in our language; his most recent translation is
Ikkyu Sojun (1394-1481): A Handful of Poems. He has also translated

Latin American poetry for Japanese people and this is wonderful. And the splendid thing is that the world keeps opening up and now there are translations of Murakami Haruki, Yoshimoto Banana, Oe Kenzaburo, Ogawa Yoko, Kawabata Yasunari, Natsume Soseki, Kobayashi Issa, and of course of the classic Murasaki Shikibu.

There's no doubt that creativity lends itself to many things. This is demonstrated by Pablo Soler Frost in his *Cartas de Tepoztlán* [Letters from Tepoztlán]:

Dear Friend:
Tepoztlán is a village [. . .]. The great slope of the central plateau ends there, in those lands, descending with some amazing stone turrets of basalt and *tepetate*. Above, the vegetation is like what's on the plateau: *oyamel* pines, citronella, beeches. As you descend, the subtropical vegetation of the Mountain appears, like coffee; but there are also apple trees and, in the valley, there are lemon, plum, and jacaranda trees. The layout of the town, nestled in the valley, is an eccentric grid: the foothills have prevented the construction of straight steps or streets [. . .]. We're in a time of drought; and we can't hope for rain until May or June [. . .]. The hills are a copper ring that encircles Tepoztlán, in such a way that, if it were extended, we'd experience the horrible phenomenon of being trapped, like tigers or adventurers of past centuries, in a ring of fire and smoke.[6]

Those letters are written to an imaginary friend in Japan. And they're written with the subtlety with which a Japanese person would describe his own landscape. The narrator understands the soul of his recipient and for that reason writes to him in a Mexican language that breathes with a Japanese air. There are also scholars in Mexico who have published valuable studies of the Japanese language, culture and economics, among them, Amaury García Rodríguez, Virginia Meza, Tanaka Michiko, Alfredo Román Zavala, and Miura Satomi. Even Carlos Monsiváis himself ended up writing about Japan and unfortunately left "The Cloaked Samurai" unpublished, but what are we going to do?

And if there are painters in Japan who dedicated themselves exclusively to describing the Mexican people and countryside, there

---

6 *Cartas de Tepoztlán* by Pablo Soler Frost. Mexico: Era, 1997. pp. 11-12.

are also Mexican artists who represent aspects of Japanese culture like the paintings of Fernanda Brunet, inspired by the *manga*, the *geishas*, and *sumō* of Yishai Jusidman, the "Finale" map of Japan of Pablo Vargas Lugo, and Edgar Orlaineta's plastic sculptures of popular personalities. And the art of Dr. Lakra (Jerónimo López Ramírez) makes me queasy because of its incredible tattoos but he is an exceptional draughtsman.

There's a belief that during the reign of Toyotomi Hideyoshi, more than 400 years ago, a Mexican ship wound up in the province of Chiba, Japan. And thanks to the help of Shōgun Tokugawa Ieyasu, the ship was able to return to Mexico without any problems. People say that during the same reign of Shōgun Tokugawa, Masamune, one of the leaders of the province of Sendai, sent his emissaries to Rome, but through Mexico. The leader of the delegation was Hasekura Tsunenaga and it's thought that he was the one who brought the Japanese painters, the same ones who were commissioned to paint the mural of the twenty-six martyrs of Nagasaki that was discovered in the Cathedral of Cuernavaca. And although Japan closed its doors to the world for more than 200 years, the Japanese feel great pride over the fact that when the country regained contact with the West, Mexico was the first country with which it signed a bilateral treaty. Besides that, the first Japanese emigrants arrived first in Mexico, then went on to other countries in Latin America.

There are many Japanese scholars who have dedicated their entire lives to researching Mexico. They are truly tireless, and there are so many of them. Although I confess that I personally like the work of Kato Takahiro on popular culture and that of Takayama Tomohiro on history. There are also those who study Teotihuacán and the indigenous people, like Sugiyama Saburo, Kuroda Etsuko, Kobayashi Munehiro, and Ochiai Kazuyasu. And on art, the studies of Kato Kaoru are particularly interesting. Mexico not only has been an endless source of inspiration and of study but also an important country in economic terms. In the seventies, Mexico was the second biggest importer of Japanese products; the first was the United States. Thus, during the terrible economic crisis that devastated the country at the beginning of the eighties, Mexico was very important for the Japanese stock market. Because of that and the relationship between the two countries, interesting works on politics have emerged, such as those of Tsunekawa Keiichi.

There is so much to learn from the efforts and creativity of those artists and intellectuals from both sides of the Pacific that one could very well build an enormous library with their works and call it: *Mekishiko to Nihon (Mexico and Japan)*. Or: *Nihon to Mekishiko*. Here the order isn't as important as the mutual respect and real tradition. A couple of months ago I read *El jardín japonés* [The Japanese Garden] by the young Mexican Antonio Ortuño. In the title-story, a neurotic heir tries to recover a love from his childhood. When he finally gets together with the girl, their meeting takes place in the Japanese garden of his house, the most serene place in that setting . . . There's no doubt that there's a huge contrast between the serenity of the Japanese gardens and the violence in most of the stories in the collection. But it's a well-written book; it's a mirror of life. As I read it, I couldn't stop thinking about the *manga* I enjoyed so much in Japan. And to think that novels as interesting as those of Eve Gil are continuing to be published. How marvelous!

Okuribito
(Departures)

In 2008, I'd planned to visit Kimiko. I thought about surprising her: in short, I'd arrive, knock on the door, and there she'd be, I thought. But one afternoon, twelve days before my departure, I came across an e-mail from An, my friend from years back who now lives in Tokyo. Her message said something like this: "Kimiko has died. Her soul rests in Heaven. Forgive me for not telling you sooner. It happened four months ago. The last time I saw her I barely recognized her, she was so sick." It was the worst news I'd ever received in my life. I left the screen as it was and ran to the bathroom. My daughter Lizeth was taking a bath. With all the strength I had left, I began scratching the shower-curtain. I wanted to tear it to shreds. I wanted to speak but I couldn't. She thought I was having a heart attack and got out of the tub, naked and lathered with soap, to hold me up. I was moaning horribly. At that moment I remembered what my father once told me when I'd angered my mother: "When your mother dies, you're going to howl like a dog." That's how it was. I cried over her death as I'd never cried for anyone. Toshi-chan had died five years before that. He'd also died of cancer. In a way, his death was tragic because he had always been a healthy man without problems. Besides that, because of his prestigious job, he'd saved all he could so he could have a healthy and dignified old age. As soon as he retired, he got very sick and died shortly afterwards. "I would have liked Toshi-chan to have lived longer," Kimiko's brother told me years later. To put it simply, everything ends in this life. Now I see why my father liked the song "Camino de Guanajuato" [The Road to Guanajuato] so much.[7]

More than a year passed before I completely recovered my strength. I knew I had to go to Japan to visit Kimiko's grave; it was something I needed to do. I returned to Nagoya and stayed in a *ryokan* or *posada*, an inn. The few people I knew who'd remained in the city had already moved away, something uncommon among Japanese people because before they never moved just like that. I never felt so lonely in a city. No, that's not true. To tell the truth, I also felt that abandoned in Mexico City when my mother died. You feel an orphanhood that penetrates your throat and chest. Not even food tastes like anything. Not even music sounds like anything. You see the bells swinging but don't hear them. And no matter how much you kneel in church and no matter how many candles you light, you feel as if your tongue has been cut out. So many things you'd like to say and . . . your tongue feels scalded. Lopped off! In Nagoya I began to roam the streets, the park and the neighborhoods where we'd lived but my body felt half-asleep. I walked till I had my fill, but aimlessly. Then I remembered the day when I woke from a dream in which a *tejocote* skin was stuck to the roof of my mouth. And to think that on those same streets, years before, I'd missed *ahuehuetes*, pepper trees, jacarandas, rue, Christmas and its *piñatas*. To think that at that time I would have given anything to taste quince, *jícamas*, and *chico zapote* fruit there. To think that over there I would have so missed hearing marimbas, accordions, and *serenatas*. To think that over there I used to remember the games I played as a girl with lizards and *ajolotes*. To think that over there I wanted to smell fried *muéganos*, *chicharrones*, and avocados. To think that over there I missed the *alamedas*[8] with their fountains, balloons, and whistles. To think that over there I missed the voices of the street vendors, the organ-grinders and the singers. And my need to hear words, sayings, slang, and malapropisms! How I longed to take refuge in my own language but I felt tethered by silence. I was tongue-tied and I only heard a shattered language, a dead language.

---

7   José Alfredo Jiménez's "Road to Guanajuato" is only one of many famous songs that still enjoy enormous popularity in Mexico as well as elsewhere in Latin America. The song opens as follows: "Life isn't worth anything / life is worth nothing, / it always begins with weeping / and with weeping it ends; / because of that in this world / life is worth nothing."

8   In Mexico, *alamedas* are large squares with trees, grass, benches, fountains, gazebos, and statues.

I located Nao-chan (Imamura Naohiro), Kimiko's brother. He and his wife, Imamura Mari, took me to their new house; they wouldn't allow me to remain alone in a *posada*. They knew me well. In fact, at one time I'd worked for them. Because of that above all they felt obliged to protect me. This is very Japanese; bosses are very paternalistic. They treated me like a teenager once again, and in the days we spent together, Mari never tired of knitting me sweaters, gloves, and caps. What amazing tenderness. They were truly surprised that I had traveled there just to visit Kimiko's grave. In their house they had a room just for the *butsudan*, an ancestral altar approximately a yard wide and more than a yard high located in the center of the room. It was made of black lacquered wood and had a gold-plated Buddha. On the left-hand wall there were three photos: one of Kimiko, one of her mother (whom I'd had the pleasure of meeting) and one of her father. The three had all died at 70 years of age. Kimiko's brother and his wife began speaking to the deceased as if she were present: "Kimiko, look who came to see you. Look at her, it's Araceli, she's here." An ineffable daze came over me, something I'd never experienced before. Then I kneeled before the altar, rang the bell, prayed to her and lit an incense-stick, as was done there. They told me that every day they offered them a small dish of steaming rice. In a way, I'd been a witness of what the dead mean to the Japanese. How couldn't I know that if my birthday is the Day of the Dead in Japan! Well, officially it's from July 13 to July 16 but in many provinces they celebrate it from August 13 to August 16. On those dates everyone used to travel home as religiously as we Mexicans do on Mothers' Day. In accordance with one of their beliefs (their faith is a mixture of Shintoism and Buddhism), it's assumed that the souls of the deceased return to visit their families for three days. So that their souls don't get lost, on the 13th, they hang lanterns around their houses to guide them. Whenever possible, each family pays a priest to visit the grave or ancestral altar of their home. They offer flowers, incense, cookies and also sweets to the dead. And to entertain the souls that have returned to the world beyond, in the afternoons, they put on folk dances and at night, a shower of fireworks bursts against a background of fireflies. On the third day they put candles or lamps on little paper boats and send them out on the water. That splendor made me weep. It looked like Janitzio on the Day of the Dead.[9] It's

---

9   Janitzio is a small island in the state of Michoacán, Mexico. The celebration there on the Day of the Dead (November 2) is almost magical. Since antiquity, fishermen have celebrated their dead with thousands of candles and *veladoras*; with dances,

believed that at that moment, the spirits return to Heaven.

The ancient Japanese used to believe that the dead went away to another world to continue living this life and that the funeral was only a ritual to prepare them. For that reason, they occasionally still dress them as if they were pilgrims on a boat, where they even put money to "pay for" the boat that will carry them to the next life. They also adorn them with amulets, a rosary in one hand, a cane in another, white socks and straw sandals. Funerals are elaborate and it's expected that those who attend will pay a good deal of "money for the incense." It's another one of those costly formalities that are a real obligation. People have to pay above all if they are morally indebted directly or indirectly to the deceased or his or her family. Money is always given in a white envelope appropriate for the occasion. Before dying, Kimiko told her brother that she didn't want him to accept money from anyone, under any circumstances. At her funeral the cheapskates and gossip-mongerers couldn't believe it, the ones who never got tired of saying that she was a miser behind her back.

Only Japanese painters can depict the mountain foliage of their country. When fall approaches, a mixture of light- and dark-green covers the landscape. On the way to the cemetery, we passed countryside and rice-fields; a faint early October sun lent a clear emerald shade to the grass. And on a steep road that climbed to the foothills of the mountains, we had to pass a giant portico that spanned the entire width of the path. It gave the sensation that we were entering a temple. When we arrived at the cemetery, there weren't doors, only more inclines, and in a little while you could make out the graves. Along the way, we stopped before a small uninhabited cottage. Nao-chan got out of the car, entered it, put money into a machine and took two bouquets of flowers. The place was empty and there were only about ten sloppy bouquets within arm's reach. It was assumed that the customer would pay if he or she wanted one or more of them. All the graves looked alike; they were made of dark-gray granite, square and rectangular, very small compared to ours. In the cemetery there were wooden buckets. Water was carried in those buckets to wash the headstones. Like most Japanese, Kimiko was cremated and was in the same grave as her parents. On the vertical burial mound more than a yard high, it read "Imamura Family" and below that, the family's coat-of-arms was beautifully engraved. On

---

rituals, and food. At night the whole island and areas surrounding it are lit up with candles and that lends an almost mystical and spiritual character to the celebration.

both sides there were granite vases engraved with bamboo leaves. All the names of the deceased were inscribed on the back of the headstone. I'd never even given a thought to the fact that I'd lived in Japan during the Showa Jidai or the Period of Enlightened Peace. Kimiko died in the following, in year nineteen of the Heisei Jidai or the Period of Peace on Earth. We left the cemetery and I saw that on the crest where the cemetery ended, some gigantic statues of Buddha were looking serenely below at the graves and the hill. *God is with you,* I thought.

But life continues and Japan continues changing. Now there are very tall buildings for housing and businesses; besides that, the neighborhood around the Nagoya Station has become fashionable. In Sakae they've installed a wheel of fortune some 15 stories high and from the top you can see the whole city. There are more museums: now you can find the Museum of High Technology Design, the Nagoya/Boston Museum of Modern Art, the Museum of Science, the Robot Museum, and Toyota opened no less than three museums since I left. There are entire buildings dedicated to the latest fashions from New York, London, Paris, and Tokyo. On the other hand, it surprised me to find second-hand clothing-shops selling name-brand items, that is, ones with designer labels. Since the economy has gotten worse, people who now can't afford to buy new clothes or accessories turn to those shops. Before, young people could wear clothes in whatever colors they wanted; married women had to be more careful about the color and neckline; and older people always dressed in black, gray, or purple. Now colors are used interchangeably. It's even fashionable to dress like young people.

People have also physically changed. Before, I used to get lost in crowds because everyone was short like me. Not now. Young people in particular are tall and have slender feet. They say that it has to do with diet because they suddenly began to eat more meat than fish. Although it's true that before there were hamburger chains, at home the consumption of meat was limited because it was so expensive. But now, like everywhere else, there are also fat and obese people, something rarely seen before. Since plastic surgery has become fashionable and is more accessible to people of modest means, women above all have their eyelids done so their eyes look bigger. There are also plenty of nose-jobs and breast enlargements. On the other hand, there are more economical alternatives: people wear colored contact-lenses and enormous false eyelashes. And in effect, their eyes look like those of the girls in *manga*, round and shiny. But what has surprised me the most is seeing women who, in a throwback almost to the sixties, wear skin-tight jeans, high-heels or boots, low necklines, long hair, and the latest style in jewelry. They are obsessed with looking young and don't necessarily subject themselves to surgery but to consuming natural products, among them green tea, juices, vitamins, fruit, fish, and tofu; in addition to this, they exercise every day. They are called *mazyo* or witches because they just don't age or at least it's not noticeable.

I don't know what happened to the poor people I saw in the Central Park in 2002 but in fact not a single one is still there. But in any case you see them now and then wandering through the streets around there. Some occupy empty lots and set up tents. They look at you without embarrassment and sometimes with an air of authority. In their tents they have portable stoves, condiments, and some even have little libraries. They get up early to search for garbage and that's how they do what they need to do. Others who don't have experience or the courage to claim a space as squatters wander throughout the city. The sad thing is that many are young. I never would have imagined that I was going to find beggars like them. On the other hand, in order to keep the city clean, as they always have done, besides their desire to protect the environment, citizens have set themselves to the task of recycling as if it were a religion. In the entrances of buildings, there are at least five designated places to put trash. As if it were a political campaign, statistics are announced through the media about the tons of garbage that are being recycled and people rejoice as if they've won the lottery. They want to be number one in recycling and have the cleanest city in Japan and in the entire world. In fact, now not even toilet paper is used (this not only has happened in Nagoya but in the entire country). Now you enter the bathroom and the toilet-seat lifts automatically. If in the process of doing your business, you don't want those outside to hear, there's a button you can push to play the sound of running water; that way, no one can know about your indisposed state. When you finish, on both sides of the bowl, there are buttons that you press to emit water that cleans and rinses you off, and air that dries you. All that is carried out with the touch of a fingertip. The Japanese bathrooms never cease to amaze me.

But *hen nahanashi*, or aside from dirty things, happily, my singing and TV idols keep producing. *Waratte iitomo*, Tamori's program, still comes on at noon every day. He is immortal, like Cantinflas was and is in our lives. He's even more active now because he has a cooking show. What energy and what creativity. Also, Kuroyanagi Tetsuko, the incredibly talented commentator and writer whom I always admired (like our Cristina Pacheco), continues producing. Matsuda Seiko, my star of all times, keeps singing without a break and unhurriedly; she also keeps launching new CDs. The fools and opportunists have tried to bad-mouth her but she doesn't let them. Like all the greats, she's self-confident and intelligent. My other favorite singers—Itsuwa Mayumi, Matsutōya Yumi, and Mikako Harumi—also keep performing. Also, Ou Yang Fei Fei, a Taiwanese singer who lives in Japan and whose song *Love is Over* I adored so much, continues singing and not only that but she has become super-attractive.

I had the opportunity to go to Nagakute, a town on the outskirts of Nagoya. I went to visit the *Takayoshi Mekishiko Bijyutsukan* or Takayoshi Museum of Mexican Art. It's the museum of the master Itō Takayoshi, the painter who loaned me that Yucatecan dress when I participated in the Sister Cities Fair in 1982. It gave me enormous pleasure that his dream had come true because he'd always wanted, with all his heart, to create a place to exhibit Mexican culture. The patio of the entrance is full of earthenware pots, stelae, and sculptures that he bought on his many trips. Aside from his paintings and those of his daughter, the artist Wada Saori, he exhibits paintings by Japanese artists who have dedicated their entire lives to painting Mexican themes. His son, Itō Hajimu, is a ceramicist and lived in Taxco for several years. His pieces demonstrate nothing less than a magnificent mixture of Japanese and Mexican art side by side. Some of his regional dresses that I'd already seen so many years before are now on display. And since he has so many, he rotates them so they can be appreciated little by little. My eyes got moist at the sight of so many Mexican artifacts and even a collection of coins. On the second floor there are paintings by Mexican and Japanese artists and a small library with art books in Spanish and Japanese. Alongside the museum is the workshop where Saori teaches techniques of Mexican textiles. "It doesn't matter what we undertake to create, whether it's painting, ceramics or textiles, in the end everything turns out very Mexican," his daughter told me. They had just returned from a trip to Santiago Pinotepa Nacional and to Santa María Asunción Tlaxiaco. They never get tired of visiting small *pueblos* in Oaxaca in spite of the fact that Master Itō is more than 80 years old and is very delicate in health. On that trip, they also visited Takeda Shinzaburo, the disciple of Itō Takayoshi who came to Mexico in 1963, the same year that he decided to live in our country. Takeda is known as the "most Mexican" of the Oaxaca artists because of the passion with which he depicts traditional Mexican culture through representations of ceremonies and festivals. As I was leaving, Master Itō gave me two books that he'd published about his paintings: *Itō Takayoshi gashū* and *Mekishiko wa gakokoro no tabi*. He also gave me a calendar that he'd designed in red and black ink in celebration of that year. It's a beautiful tiger. This year of 2010 is the Year of the Tiger, according to the Chinese calendar. Kimiko and Toshi-chan were also "tigers," as I am. The Japanese believe that when three tigers get together (although not to *tragar trigo*,[10] or swallow wheat), good luck, health, and prosperity result. I could confirm that. And this same year the City of Nagoya celebrates its four hundredth anniversary, so not just Mexico is celebrating.

My friend Maguchi Mihoko went to live in the country. No one could explain to me exactly where she was living. Sako Hitomi or An-chan now is called Ueda Hitomi because she married my old friend Ueda Akira. They live very happily in Tokyo. Hayashi Joji is also working and living in Tokyo. My great friend, the doctor Yoshitake Keiki, still has a clinic in Nagoya and continues seeing the poor and immigrants. Being rich, he always got involved with people of scant resources. In his clinic he had four assistants and worked with an enviable efficiency. Since he knew that many of the foreign workers had little money, he treated them at no charge and as if they were his own family. He ended up seeing many people from the Philippines and from other parts of Asia in his clinic. In fact, when I left Japan, I told him that I was entrusting to him "my friend" Pedro San Venancio, a Spaniard who'd come to work for Kimiko. He was from a small town near Salamanca. Pedro wasn't really my friend because we barely knew each other but out of politeness I entrusted him to Doctor Yoshitake. When Pedro fell sick, Kimiko ignored him, with her usual chilliness in those matters. The one who took care of him was my friend Yoshitake Keiki and it soon became clear that Pedro needed some procedures having to do with his heart. Doctor Yoshitake managed all that because I'd asked him to take care of him. How wonderful! What luck I had knowing such good people!

The last time I spoke by telephone with Kimiko, she told me that her legs hurt and that it was making it difficult for her to walk. She didn't tell me that she had a cancer that was taking over her entire body or that she was in a wheelchair. . . . For my part, I told

---

10   Literally "to swallow wheat"--a popular tongue-twister that begins, "*tres tristes tigres tragaban trigo. . . .*"

her emotionally that I'd recovered from a depression I'd fallen into, that I was exercising and that I wanted to write something about my stay in Japan. She became emotional and begged me to do it soon. "Come back to Japan soon. And take me from here to some other place, wherever you want," she asked. Several weeks later she sent me a box with sportswear; it came complete with pants, jackets, and T-shirts in my favorite colors. She also sent me a long peach-colored skirt and blouse. In the middle of her terrible and painful condition, she sewed them with kimono fabric that she'd treasured since her youth. I didn't return on time. I didn't learn about her illness, either. It caused me such pain that my own mother in Mexico, seeing me suffering like that, set herself the task of saying a rosary for Kimiko every day, every day until she died that May 23, 2009. After visiting Kimiko's grave, I had to get to Tokyo. Yes, to Tokyo, to Tokyo. I had to board the plane, to lose myself in the clouds and forget everything, at least for a while.

"You look Japanese," people often tell me everywhere. How could I not look that way, even if I don't carry Japan in my blood, I carry it in my heart!

With Itō Takayoshi outside the *Takayoshi Mekishiko Bijyutsukan* (Takayoshi Museum of Mexican Art), 2010.

Araceli (center) at the United Nations Headquarters, New
York working as a Spanish-English-Japanese tour guide, 1989.

Lecturing on Latin America and technology at
The University of Tokyo, 2014.

With Tokyo University faculty after the lecture, 2014.

Feature article in *The Ryukyu Shimpo* highlighting the author's lecture on Cuba in the 21st century; Okinawa, June 26, 2015.

About The Author

Araceli Tinajero was born and raised in Mexico City. Before joining The City College of New York and the Graduate Center, she taught Japanese at the University of Wales and Spanish and Latin American literature at Middlebury College and Yale University. She is the author of *Orientalismo en el modernismo hispanoamericano* and *El Lector: A History of the Cigar Factory Reader*. Her editions and co-editions include *Cultura y letras cubanas en el siglo XXI, Orientalisms of the Hispanic and Luso-Brazilian World, Exilio y cosmopolitismo en el arte y la literatura hispánica, Technology and Culture in Twentieth Century Mexico*, and *Handbook on Cuban History, Literature, and the Arts*.

About The Translator

Daniel Shapiro's publications include the poetry collections *The Red Handkerchief and Other Poems* (2014) and *Woman at the Cusp of Twilight* (2016), and, in addition to *Kokoro*, two other translations: Tomás Harris's *Cipango* (2010; starred review, *Library Journal*) and Roberto Ransom's *Missing Persons, Animals, and Artists* (2017). Shapiro has received translation fellowships from the National Endowment for the Arts and PEN. He is a Distinguished Lecturer at The City College of New York, CUNY, where he serves as Editor of *Review: Literature and Arts of the Americas*.

CPSIA information can be obtained
at www.ICGtesting.com
Printed in the USA
FFOW05n1816131217